CONCILIUM
Religion in the Seventies

CONCILIUM

New Series: Volume 2, Number 10: Liturgy

POLITICS AND LITURGY

Edited by
Herman Schmidt and
David Power

Herder and Herder

1974
HERDER AND HERDER NEW YORK
815 Second Avenue
New York 10017

ISBN: 0-8164-2576-0

Library of Congress Catalog Card Number: 73-17910

Printed in the United States

CONTENTS

Editorial

IN Latin America, a particular type of liturgical service is commonly known as a Mass of Protest. At the World Conference on Salvation Today, organized in Bangkok by the World Council of Churches in December 1972–January 1973, the participants in a service of worship prayed for those mothers whose children today are "no more" because of exile, torture, hunger or brutal death. The Roman Missal carries a formulary for a Mass for Peace. These are but some of the many facts that one could enumerate to show that in practice communities do link liturgy and politics.[1] Yet on a theoretical level the bringing together of the two words sometimes provokes mystification, if not downright distrust.

In deciding to edit an issue of *Concilium* on this theme, the first problem was to determine the meaning of the word and the reality of "politics". A first tentative step in this direction seemed to be suggested by the word's etymology: by definition or derivation, politics concerns the social welfare of the *polis*, and is the responsibility of all. Yet one is immediately stopped short by the reminder that in ancient Greece, where this idea was born, only a small section of the inhabitants constituted the *polis*, i.e., those recognized as free men.

We most certainly understand politics to refer to the total public

[1] An exposé of what is in fact being done is presented in the first article of the issue by H. Schmidt. It is complemented by an historical article by H. Meyer, from which we see that there has always been relevancy in the question about liturgy and politics.

welfare, with due regard for the position and good of every section and every member of society. As such, it is exercised on a local, national and international level. How much, however, on any of these levels it can involve the responsible action of all the people is a question to which there is no facile answer.

Not every form of work for social and public welfare constitutes politics. More specifically, it describes that *exercise of power* which controls public welfare and progress. It is the reality which counts in the first instance, so that we have to be careful not to prejudice our treatment of it by giving a normative definition, i.e., one which already contains a value-judgment. Needless to say, the exercise of politics or the control of power in society raises the question of its legitimization. Every ruler, or body of rulers, wishes to ground his authority in some kind of right. Every community tries to determine procedures which govern the taking, holding, renouncing, transmitting and exercise of power in its midst. There are in effect many different forms of justification, as well as many different instances wherein the legitimacy of the power-holder is contested, either on the grounds which he himself put forward or on grounds which are suggested as more equitable than those actually in use.

The question for the Christian is whether the gospel bears any reference to the exercise of power in society, and whether this enters into his horizons when he is at prayer. The first part is not the particular issue for this number and has been treated elsewhere in *Concilium*.[2] If we presume a positive answer to it, what is to be said about the second? The answer is far-reaching, because it involves a stance on the nature of salvation and on the relation between faith and world, between prayer and daily service, between the kingdom of God and the kingdoms of this world.

The New Testament vocabulary indicates a close affinity between the realities of service, power and authority on the one hand, and worship on the other. Granted that the first three words refer in the first instance to activities within the church community, the question follows as to whether or not they also have a bearing on worship when referred to the totality of human

[2] Cf. *Concilium*, March 1973 (American edn., Vol. 83).

living. This is particularly important if we recall that the lordship of Christ is described as cosmic, exercised over every worldly reality and principality and power. Can liturgy then which celebrates the lordship of Christ fail to refer to the powers of this world? Or put in other words, must not Christian liturgy have some bearing on the exercise of power in social matters if these are to be in turn transformed into a Christian *diakonia*, a service of man which is also a service and a worship of God?

The symbolism of power seemed to be of great importance in discussing our question. Since politics is the control of power in society, the ways in which liturgy uses symbols of power has much to say in forming images and concepts of power which Christian peoples bring to bear on political questions. At the same time, it did not seem wise to view this exclusively from the standpoint of Christian worship. Within the broader context of the way in which man symbolizes the forces and powers at work in his world, it is possible to see how a Christian community can take account of the totality of forces which enter into the making of man's world, and how he can interrelate them. This puts a very pressing question to those who would like to find a form of escapism in prayer and ritual. It is not uncommon today for people to seek salvation or freedom from the demands of a technicized world by escaping into a world of nature, joy and innocent love. Does one, however, change the controlling forces of the world by ignoring them? Does not a symbolization of power have to find a better way of integrating these forces into a meaningful world?

Good and evil are twin concepts and opposing realities. If politics is the exercise of power on behalf of the common good, it must needs have some framework of reference within which to determine what is good and what is evil. On the other hand, salvation is by very definition the freeing from evil and the transferring of man into the good of God's kingdom. Hence the relevancy of a discussion of the symbols of evil (J. Navone). This shows the dialectic between freedom and evil. It also makes us conscious of the many ambiguities present in man's images of what is evil. Clearly, the symbolization of evil in Christian art and prayer is a practice in need of constant reappraisal, and has considerable effect on the deploy of forces which shape the world

of man. At the same time, because the Christian finds it necessary to refer man's evils to sin and to explain them in terms of
his relation to God, he is inevitably critical of any endeavour to
tackle the world's evils in a totally a-theistic (or even anti-theistic)
way.

The ultimate quest of sacramental service is man's freedom to
worship God in spirit and in truth. It has then to be asked what
relation there is between political freedom and this freedom in
grace. There are a vast number of ideas about what constitute the
essential freedoms of man to be preserved and respected by political powers. What stance can the Christian community take towards these in its primordial quest for the kingdom of God and
its justice? We asked J. Llopis to discuss how the homily in particular may raise the question of political freedoms within the
perspective of eschatological freedom. On a broader basis,
J. Moltmann offers some considerations on the nature of Christian celebration as a liberating feast.

We would have liked to present a fuller reflection on prayer
as the prayer of God's kingdom, based on the model of the Lord's
Prayer. We would also have liked a fuller treatment of the relevancy of the Symbol of the Father to the theme of liturgy and
politics. In the event, both these contributions proved impossible.
The concluding theological article by D. Power, presented in the
nature of a synthesis, may to some extent supply these de-
ficiencies, at least by keeping us mindful of these aspects of the
problem.

So as not to avoid the more immediately practical, J. Gelineau
gives some guidelines for practice. The bulletin by H. Schmidt
provides an interesting point of comparison, from which liturgies
may draw some lessons about the way in which to present a
world-view involving political concerns.

DAVID POWER
HERMAN SCHMIDT

PART I
ARTICLES

Herman Schmidt

Lines of Political Action in Contemporary Liturgy

THIS article offers certain comments on the lines of political action present either openly or covertly in various current liturgical forms. Many people are instinctively opposed to harnessing together politics and liturgy. That is mainly because they have a narrow or unfavourable conception of politics, and not so much that they do not know what liturgy is—there are, after all, some specialists in liturgy who are very much against this particular combination. Then too they have an objection to political and revolutionary theologies. It will become clear from what follows that the linking of politics with liturgy has not sprung from those theologies. There are of course political liturgies that give a liturgical expression to such theologies, but there is a critique of them as well—a critique based on the Bible and in liturgy, which have been, after all, and continue to be the sources of theology as a discipline.[1]

It is necessary, therefore, to explain what is meant here by "politics", taking as our starting-point the *polis* as a concrete phenomenon in both society and Christianity. It is in terms of this reality that we can define politics as a social phenomenon and summarize what is required for truly humane politics. Even in what has been said already liturgy comes in, as it were, quite automatically. Having given this introduction, we can proceed now to offer a panoramic view of the conjunction of Christian politics and liturgy in our own age. In this section it will emerge

---

[1] A source of inspiration for this article was: J. Lochman, *Perspektiven politischer Theologie* (Zurich, 1971).

that belief in the Christian revelation is the immovable point of departure for this essay and is not matter for discussion: without belief, after all, there can be no liturgy, and therefore no systematic study of it.

This article does not pretend to be the last word on the subject. It is an inquiry, a trial run, for it is moving in an area which is still developing and has yet to be properly investigated.[2]

I. THE CITY

It was Greece that gave us the humane city. Hers was an urban civilization. The miracle took place in the *poleis*, the cities, and the national pride of the Greek was directed first and foremost to his native city. What do we owe to the Greeks? Being who we are, being *human* beings. All humanism derives from them. Regulating and ordering things—that activity which is typical of the intelligence—was the distinctive passion of the Greeks. The universe, for their oriental neighbours a plaything of ruthless deities, was for them a cosmos, an ordered entity, measurable, calculable, something that could be explored and interpreted on a rational basis. In the "poleis" there was, at least for the (free) citizens, freedom, a restless inquiring spirit and intelligence sufficient to carry out every sort of political experiment, one after another: from clan-king-subject to oligarchy and, in the end, democracy, so much so that the vocabulary they used for these things is still ours today. Enough intelligence also to assimilate what could be known, to classify and systematize it, so that the foundations of geography, history, physics, anatomy, medicine, psychology, grammar, prosody, politics, logic and finally philosophy are Greek creations—foundations which we still apply and from which we still proceed even today.

From Roman civilization came the republic (and after that the

[2] O. Betz (ed.), *Das Wagnis mit der Welt* (Munich, ³1969); J. Daniélou, *L'oraison, problème politique* (Paris, 1965); A. Hebert, *Liturgy and Society* (London, 1961); H. Meyer, *Politik im Gottesdienst?* (Innsbruck, 1971); H. Meyer (ed.), *Liturgie und Gesellschaft* (Innsbruck, 1970); L. Monden, "Politiek, gebed of kontemplatie", in *Hoogland—Dokumentatie* 13 (1971), pp. 101-13; E. Philippart de Foy, *T.V., politique, confort, sport, mode, travail, et la vie intérieure?* (Brussels, 1986); R. Pibiri, *La preghiera: fuga o liberazione?* (Turin, 1972).

empire), with its centre of energy in the *urbs romana*. That world empire grew out of a tiny but sturdy state of farmers and soldiers with a strictly ritualistic religion, a lofty civic and family morality and a sense of immediate reality. Besides his heroic past, the Roman of the imperial age possessed yet another moral resource: the Hellenistic culture which had been imported since the time of Cicero, taken over in a remarkable selection and translated into Latin.

The coming of Christ changed the whole aspect of late antiquity and the culture of the time. In the society of the end of the first century there appeared, to the astonishment of Jew and pagan alike, a third race: the type of people who in Antioch had been given the name of Christians. The appearance they presented has been portrayed on countless occasions and is familiar to us all. What distinguished them from everyone else was the Lord, always the Lord. They were well named "Christians": their world was that of the Christ of Scripture, their city not Athens or Rome or the by now devastated Jerusalem, but the kingdom of God, which had come down from heaven to earth and to which, founded on Jesus Christ the corner-stone, living stones were being added, for the completion of an eternal Jerusalem on the last day. This is the city celebrated in a halting Latin by an anonymous poet at some time between the sixth and eighth centuries, in the hymn *Urbs Ierusalem beata*. The Church of God on earth is an antitype of the heavenly Jerusalem, *quae construitur in caelis*. It is apocalyptic. It is a mystery like the Incarnation of the Word of God, outsurge and implementation of the Incarnation, an epiphany, a process. At the Renaissance not only was the Latin of this hymn turned into a classical Latin, but its theology too was inverted. In the humanistic *Caelestis Urbs Ierusalem*, the city does not descend from heaven to earth but the "terrestrial" Church rises up, a "celestial" city from the earth to the stars, *quae celsa de viventibus saxis ad astra tolleris*. The glory of the Church-on-earth is celebrated and is not regarded as the antitype of a transcendental reality. The humanistic hymn is an allegory, rhetorically sublimating the earthly cities of the ancient cultures, Athens, Rome and Jerusalem, into a heavenly utopia. After Vatican II, Paul VI's breviary replaced the *Caelestis Urbs Ierusalem* of Pius V's breviary with the original *Urbs beata*

Ierusalem, which signalized a return from scholasticism and Renaissance to biblical and liturgical theology.[3]

In our own time the world is becoming, so to speak, a tremendous metropolis, constructed by autonomous Man for his earthly happiness. That welfare is being worked for with unprecedented vigour. When things go wrong with this gigantic undertaking, Man is not cast down but shows exuberant daring. With the full force of all the energies released in him, he is going to bring about, through science and technology, what for his forefathers was a utopia. Despite the catastrophe of world wars and the spectacle presented by the methods of totalitarian systems his faith in technology and in automatic progress persists. His metropolis is a product of *hybris*, of rash pride. Metropolitan man appears to have settled accounts with his past. Any recollection of it becomes a *memoria subversiva*, a critical overturning of what was in order to do what is and what makes free. His unbridled desire to play at being Superman is heedless of the Greek city, where the ideal of human personality was *sophrosyne*, wisdom: a mixture of knowledge, a sense of moderation, self-knowledge. His agglomerates of masses bear no resemblance to the Roman Empire with its ideal of the *virtutes humanae*, the humane virtues; nor apparently does it give him pause to realize that these cultures have remained lofty human ideals without any ultimate realization.

Again, the modern metropolis cannot accept the ideal of the Christian city as capable of being realized, because it encounters Christianity in divided and anaemic churches, devoid of all magnetism: there is no longer an *exodus* from Egypt to the Promised Land, but one from the churches to the metropolis. Christianity as a process in history seems to have been sidetracked, now that Pope John's charisma has been snuffed out and the driving force of ecumenism paralysed. The Christian city is not a mass-metropolis, as the astronomical figures presented by statistics would have us believe. Its strength lies hidden now in a kind of dying, which as John the Evangelist has said, can be a promise for the future: "Unless a corn of wheat falls into the

[3] The foregoing has been prompted by F. van der Meer, *Atlas van de westerse beschaving* (Amsterdam, 1951), and A. Mayer, *Die Liturgie in der europäischen Geistesgeschichte* (Darmstadt, 1971).

earth and dies, it will remain alone; but if it dies, it will produce rich fruit" (Jn. 12. 24). For the metropolis the still persisting "futility" of Christianity is a quaint relic of the past without significance; for death and life are irreconcilable. Classical humanity and Christian faith are nowadays lived out in the experience of individuals and groups—in diaspora, of millions— and no longer automatically handed on from above or from inside, as a matter of convention, to the multitude. There a nostalgic longing for the heavenly Jerusalem obstinately survives and finds a response, when it is able to express itself in a language that is understood today, that is, in a language that does not sound a triumphalist note but is cautious, tentative, hopeful and questioning and able to draw a response from what is dormant in those who amid the anonymous mass of people are still persons with a name and possess something that everyone is really looking for. Amid the mass production of songs which glorify, bemoan and damn the metropolis, in the liturgy too sounds are heard—sounds inspired particularly by the psalms— travelling from and into the distant places.

II. THE SOCIAL PHENOMENON OF POLITICS

The word *polis* was not taken over into the Latin. Because the Roman ruled the world, *orbs*, he called the city of Rome, centre and summit of the world, *urbs*. Of course we do find in Latin *politia* for *politeia* and *politicus* for *politikos;* but there was a preference for rendering these Greek words (as well as *urbs*) by *civitas, civis, civilis. Politeia* means citizenry, republic, organization, homeland, state, form of government. Our word "police" is related to the idea of "politeia": the body equipped with power to protect the community and maintain order. *Politikos* is primarily civic, civil, serving the well-being of the citizens, pertaining to the state, and then, cultured, civilized, constitutional.

Well known are the passages in the *De Civitate Dei* where Augustine links politics with theology: *genus (theologiae) mythicon, physicon, civile* (6, 5); *theologia fabulosa, naturalis, civilis* (6, 7 and 8); *tres theologias quas Graeci dicunt mythicen, physicen, politicen* (6, 12), that is, mythology—the study of the gods useful to philosophers in expounding nature—the study of

the gods venerated in the cult (worship) of the city.[4] In Latin
liturgical texts we do not find the Greek terms above-mentioned,
nor very often the Latin translations of them. We do, however,
come across a lot of synonyms.[5]

Sociologically speaking, one might define politics as follows:
Politics is a special form of social activity that needs and pursues
power, is aimed at control established and secured by laws and
seeks to manage and regulate the public affairs of the community,
often on some model of society.[6]

Every community seeks a balance between general and individual well-being. To that end models of society are projected
which may vary in character: monarchy, aristocracy and democracy, totalitarianism, liberal and socialistic systems, etc. Any
political system requires power and exercises control on the basis
of a system or institution (for instance, a constitution) sanctioned
by laws, in order to safeguard the general well-being of all sectors
in the community.

The above description of politics is an abstraction intended to
designate a social behaviour pattern. That abstraction becomes a
thing of terror, if the concept of "politics" and not *"man carry-
ing on politics"* is declared to be a real entity. In other words
politics is not something real in itself but a pattern of behaviour
in man. This is why man furnishes politics with its ethical norms.
Politics as a power outside man himself is an idol, a demon that
takes possession of an individual or a party, an inhuman dictatorship over people. We must now indicate what are the human
ethical norms of politics as a social phenomenon.

III. A Truly Humane Politics

Politics is a *human* activity (not, therefore, an impersonal,
anonymous social process imposed from outside) and also a social
activity shared with our fellow men (thus not a private affair).

[4] R. Markus, *Saeculum: History and Society in the Theology of St.
Augustine* (Cambridge, 1970).
[5] See G. Manz, *Ausdrucksformen der lateinischen Liturgiesprache bis ins
elfte Jahrhundert* (Beuron, 1941), 153-6. *Sacramentarium Veronense* (ed.
Mohlberg), 271, 361, 550, 706, 779, 1190, 1197, 1353.
[6] H. Schoeck, *Kleines soziologisches Wörterbuch* (Freiburg, 1969),
p. 263.

Politics is pretty much an affair of morality as well, and so is bound up with the nature of man, willed and created by God, as that nature finds its normative expression in natural law and natural right (or justice). Without a basis in morality and justice, politics gets perverted into the capricious exercise of power, vested interest or profiteering.

The aim of politics is to bring about the general well-being of the community, as it exists concretely. Not, therefore, just welfare and the pursuit of private or group interests. These may of course assert their claims within the broad area of the general good and can thus play a legitimate role in politics. Give and take is something that no community can do without.

Politics is necessary in all situations experienced by man, for instance, in the family, society, state, religions, churches, judicial organs, economy, labour associations and in all the other innumerable groupings. The idea of politics is not restricted, therefore, to the state with its political parties. The social and economic interests of the many sectors and classes who through research, labour and services further the well-being of the community are given special attention in the modern metropolis. The class struggle is not a thing of the past, for social and economic justice has not as yet been attained for all who support production and provide services. To the extent that production is being taken over by machines, productive manual labour is decreasing and the provision of services increasing, so that there is a tension and a conflict between industry and consumption. Hence a new form of class struggle, social and economic unrest. The community pursues a political line of action to try to achieve a social and economic equilibrium between the jostling sectors and areas of labour.

Politics aims at putting into practice realistic values and ideas worked out in a model or programme. Politics is at the service of truth, of what is good, of reality. It strives after an objectively justifiable end. Utopias, ideologies and reveries about the future are not political goals, but are simply beating the air. Without a solid basis and settled guidelines, politics becomes a power game, a paralysing obsession with legalities.

The view that politics entertains of society is grounded in a view of man. Both refer to an antecedent, determining principle, so that our view of the world plays a crucial role in politics. The biggest problem of modern society is the co-existence of so many and such diverse views of the world which are often diametrically opposed and as complexes cannot possibly be brought into unity or made to act in concert. After long and wearisome political negotiations, agreement on a few points may be reached and this may afford a temporary solution and a breathing-space until the next crisis comes to a head. The polarization continues, suspicion is not allayed, the struggle for power and domination escalates and violence and anarchy flare up. The notion that each and every view of the world is permissible in a single society is not a political stance, but degeneration and anarchy. The imposition by political *force majeure* and coercion of a single view of the world, whatever its character (Christian, liberal, fascist, socialist or communist), is a form of dictatorship, engenders resistance and counter-violence and may well end in civil war. Under the threat of mankind's complete destruction the political game has to go on being played, in order to save, from day to day, what can be saved. It resembles a "win or lose" type of sport, a tussle for the cup between sides which without opponents could not carry on. However much politics today may be vilified, it is the one and only plank that enables us to maintain, by hook or by crook, a temporary equilibrium. Thus all who call for freedom, justice and peace are able to go on living with hazards and conflicts, without entertaining illusions about a future of untroubled peace just around the corner, in which, the work having been finished, we need dirty our hands no more.

IV. CHRISTIAN POLITICS AND LITURGY

In the *Urbs beata Ierusalem* politics is a superior kind of reality, on the analogy of politics in this world. That city is a family, of which the Father is *almighty*, the Son the *Lord* and the Spirit the *Unity*. The prayers of the liturgy and sacramental actions are contained in a doxology: *ad Patrem omnipotentem— per Dominum nostrum Iesum Christum qui vivit et regnat—in unitate Spiritus Sancti*. In the doxology, earthly politics becomes a constituent part of the divine politics, and becomes so through the God-man, Jesus Christ. Our freedom, justice and peace do not remain an unattainable goal, but are an eschatological reality in Jesus Christ. The city of man becomes the city of God. Our power (*force majeure?* coercion?) becomes a being able (*posse*), in the total power of the Father, maker of heaven and earth, our ruling (dominating?) becomes serving in the dominion of the Lord, servant of God (*servus Yahweh*) and servant of the servants (*servus servorum*), our struggle between classes and interests becomes a loving, human solidarity in the Spirit who makes us one (*Veni, Sancte Spiritus, reple tuorum corda fidelium et tui amoris in eis ignem accende*).

This is the outlook which animates a Christian politics, summed up here in few and therefore inadequate words, but elaborated in the liturgy in a wealth of words, images, songs, movements and symbolic actions which serve to realize the deepest aspirations of man. In the liturgy, man experiences himself as a mystery in which is experienced the mystery of God. For man, the mystery of man is the first and fundamental mystery. If he himself does not live as mystery, then he shuts himself off from everything that is mystery. In the modern metropolis, the aim is to establish a notion of man that can be explained and realized experimentally, one to which mystery is alien. In every discovery, achievement and exploitation on the part of metropolis-man, the liturgy is able effectively to manifest the mystery and bring it to consciousness—man discovers what is already, man utilizes what has been made already, what man calls *new* is new for him but not new in itself (there is nothing new under the sun). The liturgy penetrates to the very heart of nature—it is gift (*donum*) and creature (*creatura*). Once man has the gift of insight, then he knows himself to be creature, gift and mystery.

In celebrations of liturgy, the crucial aspect is man and not liturgical books and manuals of instruction, just as the point about politics is not systems but man himself. The basic implication of liturgy is still service for and of the people. Where the city is Christian, the liturgy runs in a descending line from God to it, for the gates stand wide open and there is nothing to interfere with communication between heaven and earth. Where the city is non-Christian the liturgy has to proceed the opposite way—to start with the opening of the gates and the restoring of communication, so that God can come inside. This also applies to

Christians who are plunged day in and day out into the life-style of the metropolis, which does violence to their life as Christians. Even into bishops' palaces, parsonages and monasteries the mentality of the metropolis forces its way through. That is why the *actio liturgica* must first open up man in an anthropological, horizontal and immanent plane, so as in that way to afford access to the theological, vertical and transcendent power and dominion of God. The point of departure is nature as creature, earthly reality as gift, man as mystery, and the terminal point he who creates and gives and performs miracles. There is something in the argument that metropolis-man must find it easier to pray the Lord's Prayer back (*Libera nos a malo*) to front (*Pater noster qui es in caelis*). This is not so unliturgical as one might think, for in the Mass there is a special elaboration of the *Libero nos a malo* in the embolism.[7]

The words and actions of the Vatican II liturgy are well suited to the situation of metropolis-man. "Godly" Latin and the "angelic" Gregorian chant are no longer obligatory, for all languages and kinds of singing are judged worthy. In the Mass, the great doxologies are used only in the collect and at the close of the eucharistic prayer, while the prayers over the offerings and after communion have short doxologies (e.g., *Per Christum Dominum nostrum*). The end of the prefaces (*Et ideo*) often follows a short version instead of the lengthy one with the choirs of angels. At the same time the ceremonies have been simplified. These examples illustrate a shift of emphasis from God highly exalted to the God who dwells among men in Jesus Christ.

It is of importance that Scripture, including the books of the Old Testament, has been given a paramount place in all liturgical observances. Experts in exegesis and liturgy have ensured that the unadulterated proclamation of God's Word in Scripture would touch off a revolution not only in the liturgy but in the Church. Scriptural proclamation in the liturgy has a hermeneutics of its own. The liturgical community reads and listens to the Scriptures not as books furnishing unrelated information about the past of God's People. It is God himself who by way of the

[7] P. Penning de Vries, "Gebed achterste voren", in *Streven* 22 (1968), pp. 187-90.

Scriptures and quite concretely addresses the local congregation actually present, and through its history in the Old and New Testaments arouses the listening and reflecting person to redemptive action for the completion of the kingdom of God. In other words, the reading of Scripture is aimed at concrete action in the world of here and now; that world must recognize itself in the Bible in order to repent and build up a community founded on the gospel.

The readings from Scripture in sacramental observances are aimed at the creation of a course of Christian action, not just inside the church building but outside it as well. Hence some such observances are to be desiderated in "profane" areas, e.g., private houses, factories and places of work, camps and public squares.[8] In the eucharistic celebration, the paschal mystery (the Lord's passing by, his passage) is not only proclaimed but felt to be a catholic, that is, universal action, whence the name of the eucharistic prayer *Canon Actionis*, norm of action. That action begins with a sacrificial disposition and strengthening meal and is continued in the exodus, the movement out into the world, as the *Traditio Apostolica* so pregnantly expresses it at the close of the eucharist: *Festinet unusquisque operam bonam facere,* let everyone hasten to perform a good work.[9]

The bare word of Scripture will not do in the liturgy; for we do not find in Scripture a cut and dried solution to our problems. Running through Scripture we can see solutions in the sense of guidelines but not of fully worked out patterns of conduct. It is in Christ present in our midst that we look for such a pattern. Thus the Scripture readings in the liturgy are set within a surround of *didascalia* and followed by a homily, a confession of faith and prayers of the faithful. In these elements Christ is concretely operative by way of those who are the ministers of his Word to the people here and now assembled. They project concrete patterns of conduct in the context of faith in God, in the hope of ultimate perfection and through love for God and his

[8] *Buitendienst. Informele samenkomsten buiten de kerkmuren* (Baarn, 1969); M. Enkrich–A. Exeler (eds.), *Kirche, Kader, Konsumenten. Zur Neuorientierung der Gemeinde* (Mainz, 1971).

[9] B. Botte (ed.), *La Tradition Apostolique de saint Hippolyte* (Münster, 1963), p. 58.

people. That the faithful should involve themselves in the homily (literally, conversation, dialogue) and in the prayers goes without saying in local congregations who live in the problematic metropolis by the Bible; they do not go in for endless theological discussions but give their experiences and voice their expectations and doubts, led by the Spirit who makes all one. The encounter of liturgy with pentecostalism and spirituality must surely be a good thing for both of them. The ritualism of liturgy and the fundamentalism of pentecostalism and spirituality would be avoided if the written biblical inspiration and the free, charismatic inspiration were to go harmoniously hand in hand together. The homily and the prayers of the faithful are certainly delicate, as they are carried out by imperfect human beings (bishops, priests and laity) and because with all of them, despite their sacramental graces, human factors can play an unhappy role; which is why a gospel-based guidance and control (*moderamen*) are necessary.

Like every other period, ours too has a certain preference for particular books and passages, for instance, in the Old Testament, the Genesis stories, Exodus, the Book of Job, the Psalms, Ecclesiastes, the book of Wisdom and the prophets (especially Amos and Jonah), and in the New Testament especially the Our Father, the Sermon on the Mount with the eight beatitudes, Christ's attitude towards the Jewish leaders, the Acts of the Apostles, the Letter of James and the Apocalypse.[10]

The system of pericopes which gives two or three readings for each day, over one, two or three years, from the Old Testament, the apostolic writings and the gospels comes into action in the seasons centred around the fundamental mysteries of the Incarnation and Easter. Then too it is useful for an understanding of the Scriptures that before each reading there is printed a brief didactic commentary, which usually summarizes the content, using biblical words, and establishes a link with the liturgical season or a feast. There is also an attempt at creating a *continuous reading* of the several books of Scripture, especially for weekdays. In the Roman Missal and Lectionary of Vatican II, forty-six "theme" Masses are included, under the title *Missae et*

[10] See H. Schmidt, *Wie betet der heutige Mensch? Dokumente und Analysen* (Freiburg, 1972), pp. 53–76.

orationes ad diversa, a number of which have a bearing on the political aspects of our society. But in the substantial part of the two books, the *Proprium de Tempore* and the *Proprium de Sanctis,* the special theme of each Mass is not indicated—and rightly so: the particular situations of the local churches and congregations are too various for them to be assigned a precise, detailed theme from one central organ. "Theme" Masses have been brought out on an experimental basis to meet certain topical circumstances and for particular groups (children, young people, the elderly, classes of people, etc.).[11] Occasionally, too, a short passage is provided to come before the Scripture readings, taken from profane literature or from very recent newspapers.[12] The idea is to make congregations aware of their Christian mode of behaviour in the diverse situations of their environments. Everyone should be ready to confront God in his personal and communal life, and God discloses himself in the salvation-history recorded in Scripture. Even where such experiments are not being made, one can discover in the various local congregations a diversity of themes, expressed in the didascalia, the homily and the prayers of the faithful. In poor parishes, people will be more concrete than in wealthy ones. In large parishes, there will be neutrality, whereas people in grass-root communities try to evolve a clear programme of action.

There is yet another experiment that one could refer to. For those church people who attend to celebrate the liturgy only on

[11] See, e.g., *Einheit von Gottesdienst und Predigt. 13 Gemeindefeiern um aktuelle Fragekreise* (Stuttgart, 1972); F. Franzen, *Motivmessen 2. Thematische Messformulare für jeden Tag* (Essen, ²1970); J. Seuffert, *Kirche auf dem Weg. Thematische Messfeiern für Gruppen und Gemeinschaften?* (Düsseldorf, ²1970); N. Kellen and H. Wagener, *Motivmessen für Kinder* (Essen, ²1972); A. Schilling, *Motivmessen 1. Thematische Messformulare für jegen Tag* (Essen, ²1970); F. Voith, *Motivmessen für Jugendliche* (Essen, 1972).

[12] Literature: see H. Schmidt, *op. cit.,* pp. 36–45; also O. Betz, *Die Welt meditieren. Texte für ein Jahr* (Munich, ⁴1971); D. Emeis, *Zoek de vrede en laat hem niet los. Hedendaagse visie op de vredesproblematiek met talrijke documenten* (Haarlem, 1971); M. Züfle, *Mensch gesucht, z. B. Jesus. Meditationen zur nachchristlichen Literatur* (Stuttgart, 1972).

Papers: A. Klausler and J. Demott, *The journalist's prayerbook* (Augsburg, 1972); K. Magiera, *Gebete aus der Zeitung* (Frankfurt, I, ³1970; II, 1971); K. Rommel, *Gebet über der Zeitung* (Stuttgart, ⁴1970).

Sundays, the Scripture readings are found to be too fragmentary: three readings fall from above into an environment which cannot possibly absorb them because the contact and communication that one takes for granted are not there. Catechesis by itself offers no way out, for the problem lies not in a lack of knowledge and pastoral commitment or concern but in the non-functioning of a system. In the Church of St Dominic (Dominicuskerk) in Amsterdam, therefore, between Christmas and Easter (the period in which one can count on a steady public), the readings and sermons at celebrations of the eucharist during 1970 covered the whole of Luke's Gospel, and in 1971 that of John. Both cycles of seventeen Sundays have been published with all·the additional texts.[13] For the study of liturgical hermeneutics, pastoralia and politics an acquaintance with experiments of this sort can be most useful.

So far as the political action of grass-roots communities is concerned, a word must be said here about these groups, which get together on an explicitly liturgical basis. They confront some burning political problem with the Scriptures and set it within their common prayer and meditation so as to arrive at a plan of action which is concrete and justifiable from a Christian standpoint. They finish sometimes with a celebration of the eucharist. This initiative is in line with what we have already been arguing above and should therefore be greeted with positive approval, because the problems of the metropolis are illuminated in a Christian fashion through listening to the Word of God and in constant prayer and meditation. It is really implementing what is recommended in the Vatican II Constitution on the Sacred Liturgy: "Bible services should be encouraged, especially on the vigils of the more solemn feasts, on some weekdays in Advent and Lent, and on Sundays and feast days. They are particularly to be recommended where no priest is available; when this is so a deacon or some other person authorized by the bishop should preside over the celebration" (35, 4).

That recommendation is being carried further than the Constitution was able to foresee. In the first place these services of the

---

[13] *Het evangelie van Lucas voorgelezen en gepreekt tussen kerstmis en pasen* (Hilversum, 1971); *Het vierde evangelie voorgelezen* ... (1971).

Word do not take their theme from the liturgical calendar but from that of current politico-social problems. Next, they are an action of the whole group (in which priests are present as well), so that they do not just entail an active participation by lay people in an action of priests, deacons or episcopally authorized laity, but are really an action of the group as a group, in which clergy and political experts and concerned lay people, starting from the basis and from within it, can exercise a leading, or rather a guiding, influence. Lastly, it is a spontaneous action prepared for by a team (spontaneity without any preparation degenerates into a confused talking-shop, with no real communication) and thus is in a sense guided and regulated from the top within the group—but not manipulated (the great danger, which has to be carefully avoided).

Obviously, the conception of the Church in these services of the Word acquire a nuance, and affirms a nuance, which is not that of the Constitution. As a result there were conflicts between officialdom in the churches, the governing authority, and the spontaneity of these grass-root communities, when the first ecumenical political night of prayer was held in Cologne in October 1968. The outcome of those conflicts has been matter for international concern and public debate and controversy—deplorably enough, and yet inevitably, in the wake of the event. Actually, both sides attacked with the same weapons, apart from the dogmatic aberrations of the group centring around Dorothy Sölle and Fulbert Steffensky. There had already been similar politically orientated services of the Word in several places, which were able to proceed quite peacefully, without any rowdy conflicts—though, as with all initiatives, even there an amount of friction occurred which nevertheless was usually overcome by skill and tact and the use of dialogue. Scripts of these political nights of prayer have been published which may be worth studying, but not imitating; for each is so concrete and "once for all" a situation that an outsider really cannot put himself within the group.[14] Just how these

---

[14] See H. Schmidt, op. cit., pp. 161-4. On the problem of grass-roots communities and politics, see R. Metz and J. Schlick (eds.), Les groupes informels dans l'Église. Deuxième colloque du Cerdic Strasbourg, 13-15 mai 1971 (Strasbourg, 1971); Alternatieve groepen in de kerk (Amersfoort, 1972).

initiatives will develop one cannot predict. Can they really have an effect on the re-christianizing of the metropolis? Or are they just a bit of salt that being strewn around here and there may, although unnoticed, add a little more savour to society?

The cross of Jesus is the central point of the liturgy. Always and everywhere the Easter mystery is celebrated in its full reality and the whole of Christian living is expressed and experienced as the way to resurrection to all eternity. Yet the eschatological vision of the resurrection never loses sight of the reality of life in this world. Our way to resurrection is the way of the cross. With the help of a political expertise the power and mastery of the cross are bringing about the ideal community of saints.

To politicize the cross, however, is to misunderstand the Christian faith. The cross has often become a symbol of aggression thinly varnished with Christianity and has even been elevated into a "Christian" imperialism. One could point here to the crusades and to medieval and modern manipulations with the cross in wars hot and cold. The worst of it was, and perhaps still is, that wealthy Christians and even wealthy churches left the socially disinherited to their wretchedness, proclaimed poverty and misery to be special graces and in so doing pointed to the cross as affording a heaven of plenty after death; they themselves, however, continued to live in a condition of worldly abundance, out of which they were able to give alms without having to impose the least austerity on their own lives. The relevance of the cross, therefore, is to man's ultimate goal; and it is not to be misused for the purpose of achieving purely mundane political ends (one might reflect at this point on the problem presented by political parties calling themselves "Christian" or "Catholic"). It is not only the Marxists who explain the cross of Jesus of Nazareth as the outcome of a political insurrection, and so as the political indictment and dispatch of a revolutionary leader of slaves.

In the liturgy, the cross opens up eschatological values to life in this world: sin and penitence, damnation and atonement, judgment and salvation, sacrifice and redemption. In this context, where the real point is man's final alienation and final deliverance, Paul wishes to know nothing else among us than Jesus Christ and him crucified (1 Cor. 2. 2).

Even though every kind of popularization that makes for a politicizing of the cross is to be repudiated, still it must not be forgotten that the cross was also a political fact: the judgment pronounced by Pilate (he is in the Creed), the superscription, "King of the Jews", that is, a pretender to messianic status and thus to the Romans a political offender, the witness of the soldier, a political figure: "This was indeed the Son of God", and so on. The sending forth of the apostles was an eschatological Exodus, not a political campaign. But the consequences of the Easter event were felt at the political level in social relations, not at first in a programmatic way, but certainly indirectly. The message of the end of all power and might, of man's radical deliverance from slavery in every form, of the breakthrough to hope, out of the clutches of fate, activated the earthly fellowship. The legendary motto of the Emperor Constantine, *In hoc signo vinces*, can be understood in a right way and a wrong one. Wrongly, in the period that bears his name, as promise of a triumph for the *corpus christianum*, as a prestige-symbol. Properly, as token of the "narrow way" of the emulative spirit of sacrifice. The politics of power and dominion is to be transformed by the cross into a political *diakonia*. For God's sake the Christian cannot withdraw from politics; for the way of the cross does not slide over this-worldly reality but runs straight through it, with all that ensues from that.

In the liturgy the dialectical counterpoint of politics and faith is expressed and experienced in every sort of key. Political engagement is inseparably bound up with faith; but that faith is not subsumed within the political domain. Politics is affected by the faith, but is not just an affair of faith without remainder, as it were. The Exodus, the history of Jesus Christ, the biblical notion of God, the idea of the covenant, the shalom-idea, the kingdom of God, the vision of the new Jerusalem and above all the cross of Christ have a political dimension but are more than patterns of mundane political action. There is an eschatological proviso attached to the biblically and politically orientated liturgy. That does not mean for the Christian, however, that he is to give politics a wide berth and be indifferent towards it. On the contrary, biblical eschatology incites us to a life of intense and sensitive "distinguishing of spirits" and requires the adoption of a stand-

point, engagement and participation in the struggle (see, e.g.,
Rom. 13. 11–14 and Ephes. 6. 10–20).

In the eschatological perspective the believer does not remain
politically neutral, but is moved to empathy and summoned to
take sides—but always with a reservation. The political plane is
not the ultimate one. Political history is not salvation-history.
Politics are linked with the last things, but are not the last things.
Political action is bound up with salvation but is not the bringer
of salvation. It is affected by the messianic story of Jesus, but is
not the messianic kingdom. To put it positively: politics is understood and practised by Christians (and so, of course, in the
liturgy) as a secular, mundane, human affair and as such is to be
taken in earnest but not in deadly earnest. Now liturgy must be
seen in the context of the gospel and not of the law, for it is in
the gospel that its true justification lies. It is inspired by the
Ultimate and not by what is next to Ultimate, but all the same
has the latter as its earthly point of departure. When this is not
so, then liturgy becomes politicized, untrue, untrustworthy: "You
are the salt of the earth. But if the salt loses its taste, with what
will it be salted? It is good for nothing any more, but to be
thrown away and trampled on by the people" (Matt. 5. 13).

Without a truly biblical and liturgical life-style, Church and
theology become politicized and thus a caricature. We cannot
make of the gospel a juridical system or constitution in the strict
sense, for it cannot be contained in canons. We are not to make a
ceremonial of the liturgy, wrapped around with rubrics and legal
stipulations, for it is the expression and experience of the liberty
of the children of God, and according to the rules of the divine
game celebrates and sings of that liberation. A political theology
that is not based on Bible and liturgy degenerates into a game of
ideas, mortifies God and betrays man.

Because the Church is in one respect a worldly reality, a church
politics is necessary. If, however, it does not stand under the
obedience of the gospel but makes the gospel serviceable to itself
as a superior model of conduct, then it is turning the Church into
a secular state embellished with bits and pieces of gospel for
ornament, a Church no longer on the way to the kingdom of
God, but proclaiming itself to be the kingdom. Christ is constantly warning us in the gospel against politicizing the Church,

by opposing the high priests, scribes, lawyers and Pharisees of a politicized Israel, and doing so for the instruction and admonition of his Church. Way over the heads of the faithful a clerical battle rages, which they understand nothing of and which plunges them into the utmost bewilderment, now that through the liturgy they are starting to think and to live according to the gospel. The way the official Church behaves is not always crystal clear, but all too often dubious. Does the Church speak and act as Church or as state? What policies lie behind it all? The communication-media, of whatever complexion, criticize, rightly or wrongly, every public move the Church makes. The disquiet of the faithful is expressed in their liturgical gatherings, not only in grass-root communities but also in parishes and more especially in continents and countries where the Church appears to have sold out to the state or wrests itself free of it, with resistance on the part of powerful Christians who want things to go on just as they are.

Church politics plays a part in the liturgy of clerical ordination. Anyone who knows his history will be aware that there are many structures of the official ministry which have been influenced by social conditions and circumstances. From the time of the Acts of the Apostles up to our own day, we see a considerable pluriformity (note, for instance, the differences between Eastern and Western churches). The choice of bishops as well as of priests by the local churches, from the very beginnings of the Church and certainly up to the Council of Trent, has been so important that one is inclined to describe it as essential and it lay under the ultimate and explicit control and ratification exercised by the liturgical congregation. In the Latin liturgy, this selection by the local congregation has become a formality. That at any rate is what the members feel and it is expressed in conflicts and protests spread throughout the world Church. This is not the place for dealing at any length with current problems in the area of Church politics, but just to complete the picture, we must at least mention them in passing.[15]

[15] See, e.g., K. Rahner, *Strukturwandel der Kirche als Aufgabe und Chance* (Freiburg, 1972). A lot of material is to be found in the one-sided and scientifically uncritical book by F. Leist, *Der Gefangene des Vatikans. Strukturen päpstlicher Herrschaft* (Munich, 1971). On episcopal consecra-

A word or two about another notion which in the course of the Church's history has become charged with controversy: the *theologia crucis*. We shall confine ourselves to what the Bible understands to be the theology of the cross. The sign of the cross (*signum crucis*) actually and symbolically combines the horizontal and vertical dimensions of the Christian faith. In Jesus Christ God shows himself as a God engaged with history, and man as a (human) being existing for God. Time and eternity, earth and heaven, salvation and well-being, City of God and city of men meet each other in the historical event of the cross. Where the cross of Jesus "is taken apart", hopeless rifts and contrarieties appear. In the "integrated" cross the opposites are linked together, but in a tension full of hazards. Viewed in the perspective of the cross, the tension between Christian salvation and earthly well-being is not the final contradiction nor a fatal breach, but it is lived and endured under the power of hope: "For we have been redeemed so that we might hope. But if we can see what we are hoping for, then hoping is at an end; do we go on hoping, by any chance, for what we already see? But if we hope for what we do not see, we long for it with patience" (Rom. 8. 24–25).

The cross of faith and the faith of the cross are the sign of a legitimate political liturgy. It is after all in liturgy that the local church, gathered together "beneath the cross", appeals and contends for the highest values and against every aberration; and this it does in words and songs evoking action and reaction.[16] In all its words and actions it evokes and empowers *metanoia*, that is, a creative reconstituting or reconceiving of all that is ossified, stagnant, half-hearted, degenerate, and so on. It is a dynamic way of conversion and reclamation, a way which slowly but surely leads to deliverance, redemption from slavery, righteousness and

---

tion and the local church, see L. Engels, "Een bisschopswijding en de afwezigheid van de plaatselijke kerk", in *Tijdschrift voor Liturgie* 56 (1972), pp. 218-40.

[16] *Bibel provokativ* (Stuttgart, 1969–1972), 4 pts; W. Gössmann, *Protestieren, Nachdenken, Meditieren, Beten* (Munich, 1970); C. Morris, *What the papers didn't say, and other broadcast talks* (London, 1971); D. Porzio (ed.), *La provocazione* (Milan, 1972); M. Tosco (ed.), *Alzo zero. Provocazioni quotidiane per vincere l'isolamento in questo mondo tutto de rifare* (Turin, 1968).

peace at the last day—but always with a repercussion in our day. An eschatological goal would indeed be a fiction, fantasy, utopia, if a foretaste of it were not realizable in our own times. It is a *via crucis* with many setbacks in our non-Christian world and in many of our Christian institutions, which are sluggish and sunk in sleep. The liturgy is also a *via crucis* of ups and downs, of stumbling and standing up once more and begging a Simon of Cyrene's help. Even the chances of resonance in the Church and the world are meagre for those liturgical congregations and groups that are politically engaged. Yet in the nineteen centuries of Christianity a blood-red line of perseverance runs on unbroken, through all mischances and disasters, down to our own day. Christ's promises have lost nothing of their power to inspire. The Christian ideal, thought out and thought through to its very roots, opens up significant possibilities for an engaged political liturgy. It is a promise, but also an obligation. We are compelled to enunciate the message entrusted to us also in its political aspect, to witness to the command of Jesus also for the problems confronting the coming world society.

Because in this article we have been evaluating the liturgy in terms of its political lines of action, the image of the Church and of society in a modern world that has come to the fore is more a negative than a positive one. And because the political focus is on improvement and perfection, attention has centred on what is bad or might be better. Yet with all its political anxieties the liturgy must continue to be optimistic. After all, its faith, hope and love look towards the Last Things, towards the final Consummation, and so it continues to rejoice and be thankful. For the liturgy, the heavenly City has begun here on earth; and so it praises God and again gives thanks. Its vision of the world pierces through to what is good and beautiful and true; and so it acclaims the works of God and again gives thanks. Its politics of furthering the well-being of the community of mankind is directed towards true joy and gladness in the metropolis, where there are an awful lot of splendid things, greater prosperity for all is possible and justice and peace are realizable ideals.

Translated by Hubert Hoskins

Hans Bernhard Meyer

The Social Significance of the Liturgy

I REMARKED some years ago that much more attention had been paid to the question of the influence of political and social factors on the liturgy than to the question whether, and to what extent, the liturgy influences social life.[1] In a subsequent study I attempted to assess the validity of the "new liturgies" appearing during the 1960s which concentrated on political topics.[2] In this article I want to consider mainly what evidence can be found to show that liturgy has influenced the life of society.

I. METHODOLOGICAL PRELIMINARIES

This approach is characteristically modern in that it implies a theoretical recognition of the possibility of socially irrelevant worship or even of a society without worship. Where there is no basis in a sociology of knowledge, as in the case of pre-scientific and pre-critical natural religions, the problem does not arise and the question cannot be asked. In such situations both the group and the individual know only one thing; that they must take responsibility in worship for "salvation", for the proper course of the world and the fruitfulness of fields, animals and men. Without worship, the world and society would fall into decay.[3] The believer in a scientific age can certainly raise the abstract question

[1] H. B. Meyer (ed.), *Liturgie und Gesellschaft* (Innsbruck, 1970), p. 27.
[2] H. B. Meyer, *Politik im Gottesdienst?* (Innsbruck, 1971); cf. also *idem*, "Politischer Gottesdienst?", *Lebendiges Zeugnis* 1/1970. See also H. Schmidt's article in this issue, "Lines of Political Action ...".
[3] Cf. M. Eliade, *Das Heilige und das Profane* (Hamburg, 1957).

of the relevance of liturgical activity to society, but he cannot deny worship either its claim to fashion or its actual influence on social life, without unfairly reducing it to the status of a part of life without real binding force.[4] Religion—and worship is its core—is all-pervasive. This fact is now again being more clearly seen as religion manifests itself in a variety of ways, even in a number of the pseudo-religious and pseudo-liturgical practices of our so-called secularized age.[5]

Determining the influence of worship on the formation of individual and social life, and communicating this knowledge, is another matter. Worship is a communicative process, not a practical activity. This means that the criteria for its validity and effectiveness are of a different order from those of correctness and success in practical endeavour.[6] In the latter it is theoretically possible to verify the connection between cause and effect in experience and indeed in repeated experiments. In worship, on the other hand, all we have to go on is institution and tradition and the faith of the community which makes the liturgy possible and lives by it. Salvation, grace and growth in faith, hope and love,

[4] The tendency to do this seems quite common in modern sociology of religion, and is probably connected with the fact that in a pluralistic society the sociologist can only study the integrating and meaning-creating function of religion and worship—or strictly, of a particular religion and its worship—in sectors. When this phenomenon of a particular group or groups is then transferred from the level of facts to that of value (which can only be done by an illegitimate switch), religion becomes a particular area of meaning alongside others, in the life of the individual and of the community. On this cf. W. Fischer, "Sinnkonstruktion. Die Legitimität der Religion in der sozialen Lebenswelt", W.-D. Marsch *Plädoyers* (see note 5), esp. pp. 206-10.

[5] See the interesting volume edited by W.-D. Marsch, *Plädoyers in Sachen Religion* (Gütersloh, 1973), in particular the contributions by W. Marhold on the social functions of religion (pp. 77–93), by Marsch on renewal of and opposition to religion (pp. 149–72) and on the theological interpretation of religion (pp. 213–30, esp. 217–19), and by W. Fischer on the construction of meaning in religion (pp. 192–212). There is a discussion of religion in critical theory as typified by Max Horkheimer by H. Przyblski (pp. 173–91), which like the longer study by H. Czuma, "Technocratie —Fortschritt—Emanzipation. Die kritische Theorie der 'Frankfurter Schule' ", *Zeitschrift f. kath. Theol.* 95 (1973), pp. 132–73, shows how the critical theory raises questions in the philosophy of religion.

[6] On the distinction between work (as purposive-rational and communicative action and work as symbolically mediated action, see J. Habermas, *Technik und Wissenschaft als "Ideologie"* (Frankfurt, 1968).

which are the primary effects of worship, cannot be perceived directly, in themselves, but only in mediation, in their effects on individual and social life. But the process by which these primary effects of worship are translated into actual features of life takes place, like all other intellectual and cultural developments, on a number of different levels. These include the language, art and social structures of a culture, which give each period its own stamp and all of which follow their own laws. Development does not take place at the same rate in the religious and ecclesiastical sphere as in others; there are dislocations[7] because attachment to tradition is stronger in the former.[8]

Even these few remarks show how delicate our task is. They also indicate that we shall have to make do in general with results from the process of mediation, since what is mediated is only accessible to faith, and not to the methods of history, psychology or sociology. This is also an appropriate point at which to ask why, as was noted at the beginning of the article, more attention has been devoted in the past to the influence of social and cultural factors on liturgy than to the influence and effects of liturgy on culture and society. Is this just an accident, or does it conceal an essential aspect of the problem?

One relatively superficial technical reason for the phenomenon may be suggested. This is that liturgical studies have been, and still are, more interested in giving a "genetic explanation"[9] of their objects of study than in considering what effects the celebration of the liturgy had on other areas of life.[10] This question was left to other disciplines.[11]

[7] Cf. Meyer, *Liturgie und Gesellschaft*, p. 31; *Politik im Gottesdienst?*, pp. 12 ff.

[8] Cf. J. A. Jungmann, *The Liturgy of the Word* (London and New York, 1966), pp. 21 ff.; H. B. Meyer and J. Morel, *Ergebnisse und Aufgaben der Liturgiereform* (Innsbruck, 1969), pp. 20 ff.

[9] See the sub-title of Jungmann's classic *Missarum Sollemnia*, "A genetic explanation of the Roman Mass", and similarly A. Stenzel, *Die Taufe* (Innsbruck, 1958), which is described as "a genetic explanation of the liturgy of baptism". The term "genetic explanation" indicates a methodological approach which typifies many liturgical studies of the past and present.

[10] This is not to say that liturgical scholars completely ignored this aspect. Jungmann's own work, for example, constantly refers to it. See note 16.

[11] Two examples are works by an historian and a sociologist, L. Arbusow,

But behind this tendency, which can be seen in many liturgical studies, there is a deeper reason. This is a particular view of the liturgy which regards liturgy, the "fountain" and the "summit"[12] of the life of the Christian Church, as conditioned in its nature by the twofold movement of "sanctification" (God's communication of himself) and "worship" (man's answer in faith), both sides of which are made manifest "by signs perceptible to the senses" in liturgical celebration.[13] These signs, the language of the liturgical meeting between man and God, exist prior to the liturgy in the structures and elements of creation, in language and the social and cultural conditions of a period. This means that liturgy is part of a one-directional process and is first influenced by these prior factors. From this point of view it is therefore legitimate and understandable that liturgical studies should first of all examine the influence of social and cultural factors on the liturgy in an attempt to understand its form and development. "The attitude to worship and its practice express the inner form of an age."[14]

The more completely the expression of a culture is taken over for the liturgy, the more closely the language and symbols of the liturgy correspond with the social features of a period, the more likely it is that celebrations of the liturgy will have secondary effects which will be felt in the life of society outside worship. When this happens the liturgy can perform its function of providing meaning and motivations which will help to shape the lives, not only of individual believers, but also of the whole believing community, and go on to influence the wider society outside this. This opens up a new field of liturgical study where, as yet, little work has been done.

These effects of the liturgy in social life occur first of all in

---

Liturgie und Geschichtsschreibung im Mittelalter (Bonn, 1951) and G. Le Bras, "Liturgie et sociologie", *Mélanges en honneur de Msgr. Michael Andrieu, Revue des Sciences Religieuses*, volume *hors série* (Strasbourg, 1956), pp. 291–304. The fields of art history and the history of ideas, comparative religion and the study of folklore, in particular, include numerous studies of this subject. Linguistic scholars have also done similar work, for example, the Nijmegen school.

[12] Vatican II, Constitution on the Liturgy, 10.   [13] *Ibid.*, 7.

[14] A. L. Mayer, "Die Liturgie in der europäischen Geistesgeschichte", *Gesammelte Aufsätze*, ed. E. von Severus osb (Darmstadt, 1971), p. 47.

those areas which show only limited traces of the influence of worship because they are most dominated by internal laws and tendencies which liturgical celebrations may support or reinforce, but not alter. These include the family, work and political and cultural life. In these areas the sociologist can, for example, investigate whether "church-goers" or "practising" Christians fulfil particular norms significantly better than other groups in the population, and this may allow conclusions to be drawn about the effectiveness of the values mediated in the liturgy. Even now, however, it is very difficult to make accurate statements about these effects, and the difficulty increases out of all proportion for periods in which sociological investigation was unknown and existing sources are very limited.

These effects on social life are hard to study, but there are others which show a clear connection with worship. We shall now turn to some of them.

II. HISTORICAL FACTS

The liturgical life of the first Christian communities, in the apostolic and post-apostolic age, took its external form firstly from Jewish forms of worship and secondly from cultic practice in the Hellenistic and Roman world. In accordance with Jewish practice, services of the word were held which were open to non-Christians and to some extent had a "missionary" character (cf. Jas. 2. 1–8; 1 Cor. 14. 23–25). Participation in the eucharist, however, was restricted to Christians. This produced a variety of rumours among pagans in the early period about the irreligious and immoral character of these celebrations, against which Christian writers had to write defences. A feature which distinguished Christian religious meetings from pagan ones was that at the Christian celebrations distinctions of social status, age and sex were largely ignored, whereas they played an important part in pagan ritual (cf. Gal. 3. 26–28; 1 Cor. 7. 14, 24; 11. 1–22; 1 Tim. 2. 1–15). Women, children, slaves, members of the most disparate social and national groups, could take part in the same worship provided only that they were believers and had not been excluded from the community for any serious public offence (cf. 1 Cor. 5). The example of Pope Callixtus (217–222) shows that

even ex-slaves could reach the highest offices in the Church. Callixtus also upheld the right of prominent Christian women to
marry slaves.

The liturgies of the word which were open to sympathizers
who were not yet members of the community probably left no
mark on life outside the Christian community, which made
them and the normal eucharistic celebrations all the more important for the community itself. It was chiefly in worship that the
attitude grew which led to a gradually sharper distinction, and
finally to a break, between Christianity and the religion of Judaism. The Sabbath was separated from the celebration of Sunday,
the Passover and Pentecost acquired a new Christian content,
and Israel's holy scriptures were increasingly interpreted in the
light of the event of Christ. As its sense of identity grew stronger,
the people of the new and eternal covenant broke both national
and ethnic restraints to transform—where it did not simply abandon them, like the Temple worship—the devotional and liturgical traditions of people of the Old Covenant. This process has
left traces in the New Testament writings, most notably in the
story of Stephen (Acts 6. 8 ff.).

In the Gentile Christian communities of the early period, acceptance of Christianity had a social significance inasmuch as it
embodied a fundamental challenge to the syncretistic polytheism
of the Graeco-Roman world. One aspect of this was participation
in pagan religion, which extended into every area of family and
public life. An early example of the conflict is the question of
eating meat offered to idols, which is discussed by Paul in his
first letter to Corinth (1 Cor. 8. 10, 14–33). For many Christians,
the decision how to behave when meat from pagan sacrifices was
served in their own family, in the houses of friends or at public
banquets became a problem of conscience. As slaves or depen-
dants of pagan masters or as members of a trade association or
dining club, should they refuse to take part in such meals or not?
In spite of his defence of Christian freedom, Paul's final answer
is: "You cannot partake of the table of the Lord and the table of
demons" (1 Cor. 10. 21).

We can already see in this the first signs of the exclusiveness of
the Christian faith and Christian worship which made the Christians of the first three centuries a group socially as well as re-

ligiously distinct from their pagan neighbours. It was this also which led to the well-known tensions between the steadily increasing numbers of Christian groups and the Roman state religion, which in turn resulted in regular local or empire-wide persecutions. In spite of this, the Christian groups continued to increase and to meet regularly for worship, which was apparently the centre of their community life, even though it could not remotely match the state worship in resources or display.

One reason for this astonishing phenomenon would seem to have been the achievement of the Christians in producing a convincing synthesis between social and community life and worship, far beyond the efforts of pagan religion.[15] Great care was taken over the preparation of applicants for baptism, and the catechumenate was given its own ritual. Contact with the Christian community was maintained through worship and teaching, and also through "sponsors" taken from the community. It was their task to direct the religious and moral life of the applicant, including his charitable activity, and give an account of it. Financial help was provided when, for example, an applicant was an actor and, because of the connection between the stage and the worship of pagan gods, had to find different work. Since the time of the apostles (cf. 1 Cor. 16. 1–4; 2 Cor. 8–9; Rom. 15. 15–28; Gal. 2. 10) it had been customary to combine the eucharist with collections for the needy and to hold special feasts (the *agapē*) for the poor. The pagan feasts of the dead were transformed into meals in memory of dead Christians and in honour of the martyrs, and the poor were invited. Gifts from members of the community supported those Christians, or whole communities, who through illness, persecution or misfortune had got

[15] On the facts mentioned in the following section, see the appropriate handbooks and dictionaries of Church history, antiquities and liturgy, e.g., A. Hamman, *Vie liturgique et vie sociale* (Paris, 1968); D. Hernegger, *Macht ohne Auftrag* (Olten, 1963); V. Saxer, *Vie liturgique et quotidienne à Carthage vers le milieu du IIIe siècle* (Vatican City, 1969); L. Biehl, *Das liturgische Gebet für Kaiser und Reich* (Paderborn, 1937); A. Bigelmair, *Die Beteiligung der Christen am öffentlichen Leben in vorkonstantinischer Zeit* (Munich, 1902); F. van der Meer, *Augustine the Bishop* (London and New York, 1962); and in addition the volumes in the series *Antike und Christentum* edited between 1929 and 1939 by F. J. Dölger, the writings of A. L. Mayer, J. A. Jungmann and T. Klauser. It is not possible to give a full bibliography within the limits of the space available here.

into difficulties, and amazingly large sums were often spent in this way. Travelling Christians, especially those in distress, could always be sure of hospitality and support at the expense of the community, whose funds were administered by the clergy. In the office of deacon, the apostolic Church had, right at the beginning, created a ministry in which liturgical and social functions were combined.

The evidence of the New Testament documents and of the post-apostolic period together shows that the Church's charitable activity was intimately connected with its religious and liturgical life. One indication of this is the language used. *Diakonia*, *koinōnia*, *leitourgia*, *eulogia*, *kharis*, *prosphora*, *thysia*, *offerre*, *oblatio*, *operari*, and so on, are all terms constantly used for social concerns, but they have at the same time a clear religious and liturgical character. This is a reflection of the way in which, in the minds of the early Christians, the sacrifices of believers were inseparable from the sacrifice of Jesus, the memory of which was celebrated in the eucharist. It was no more than a logical development from this for the clergy who served the altar to care also for the poor and the sick, the widows and the orphans, the unemployed and travellers, in short for all those who were in distress. For these all the faithful contributed according to their means when they met daily, or at least every Sunday, to celebrate the eucharist.

The facts listed here as examples go some way to explaining how strong an attraction the life of the Christian communities exerted on pagans. Worship and a morality imbued with the spirit of the gospel, which expressed itself in a broad range of social commitment, formed an impressive combination. Its impressiveness was heightened by the contrast with pagan worship, which could offer no counterpart to the moral seriousness of Christianity and seemed mainly concerned with the correct performance of ritual.

By the time of the persecutions it was becoming clear that the steadily increasing number of Christians was making it more and more difficult to maintain Christian life at the pitch at which martyrdom, if need be, was accepted as the normal implication of a commitment to the gospel through the *sacramentum* of the baptismal promise. The emotional energy of a community

waiting for the fulfilment at the end of time had long ago ceased
to shape the lives of all members to the same degree. It proved
on theological grounds to be mistaken, and in the pastoral situation ever more difficult, in fact impossible, to apply the strict
standards which zealots like Tertullian, Hippolytus and Novatian
wanted to see used against members of the community who
failed to live up to the ideals of Christian life. This development
is symbolized by the history of penitential discipline. Tolerance
was opposed, but spread, and gradually developed into special
forms for the sick and the dying, and later for heretics and members of the clergy.

As the communities grew, even before Constantine, and the
ecclesiastical organization within them and the links between
them became established, the Church became an element in public
life. It was not yet officially recognized, but it could no longer
be ignored, and the climate in which Christians lived inevitably
altered. Their life in the world came to seem less temporary.
The pressure on individuals and on the community to make
themselves at home grew stronger, and so did their sense of responsibility, not just for the approaching end, but for a happy
continuation of history. As early as Tertullian, we find the idea
that Christians pray for the preservation of the Roman Empire
to delay the appearance of Antichrist and the end of the world
(*Apol.* 39; *PL* I.468). Prayers such as this, "for all men, for kings
and all who are in high positions, that we may lead a quiet and
peaceable life, godly and respectful in every way" (1 Tim. 2. 2)
had been said in the liturgy since apostolic times, and the writers
and martyrs of the first Christian centuries regarded them as their
contribution to the maintenance and support of the empire and as
a reason for the emperor and the state to grant them toleration, if
not support. There was in fact a rapprochement in the course of
the third century between the primitive Christian Great Church
and the Roman state. It was interrupted, notably by the persecutions of Decius and Diocletian, but was nevertheless part of a
single process leading up to Galerius' Edict of Toleration in 311,
in which Christianity was given equal status with other religions
and Christians were commanded to pray to their God for the
welfare of the emperor and the state (Eusebius, *Hist. eccl.* 8, 17,
3–10).

THE SOCIAL SIGNIFICANCE OF THE LITURGY

The more Christianity became part of the political system under Constantine and his successors, the more opportunities there were for Christian values and the Christian liturgy to influence society. One example is the famous Sunday law of 321, which decreed that the courts and labourers should not work on Sundays (*Cod. Theod.* II. 8, 1a and II. 8. 1). A society until then officially pagan now began, under the influence of a minority heavily supported by the emperor, the long and eventful process of transformation into a Christian society. It is impossible to underestimate the role of the liturgy in this process, particularly when it is remembered that it was not until the Middle Ages that Christian schools appeared on any scale.

Knowledge of Scripture and Christian moral teaching continued to be acquired by believers and catechumens for the most part through worship and preaching.[16] The celebration of the liturgy also accompanied the individual Christian through his life from birth to death with its rhythm, the daily prayers and public worship, the Sunday eucharist, the seasonal ember days, the great festivals coming round year by year preceded by their period of preparation and followed by their period of celebration, the commemorations of the saints fixed in the yearly calendar, the sacraments and sacramentals. The liturgy also placed all events of importance to society in a meaningful context. It left its stamp on all of public and private life, and ensured that the people did not just know about the central mysteries of the Christian faith, but also experienced them in celebration.

It is not hard to show that when Christianity became a national Church whose membership was co-extensive with the population of the empire, when it included in its feasts and practices pre-Christian and non-Christian forms of worship, when it allied itself with political power and itself became a power in society, by adopting secular models and pagan practices, it ran the risk, not perhaps of losing its true essence, but certainly of obscuring it.[17] Not only was this danger clearly felt in the history of the

[16] See J. A. Jungmann, *The Easter Liturgy to the Time of Gregory the Great* (London and New York, 1963).

[17] See, e.g., Hernegger, *Macht ohne Auftrag*, esp. pp. 287–356; J. Baumer, H. Christoffels, G. Mainberger, *Das Heilige in Licht und Zwielicht* (Einsiedeln, 1966), G. Hierzenberger, *Der magische Rest* (Düsseldorf, 1969), esp. pp. 78–217, and the references given in these books.

Church since the fourth century, but many phenomena in the Church life of our own day have been shaped by it.

In popular piety especially, centrifugal tendencies soon developed which threatened to distract devotion from essentials. Such tendencies include, for example, the veneration of the Mother of God, of angels, saints and their relics, the celebrations of the memory of the martyrs, the innumerable patronal festivals and pilgrimages which grew up in the course of centuries, novenas, devotions, processions, brotherhoods and pious associations, the saints' days which until recently crowded the calendar of feasts, the Old Testament or even pagan and magic ideas which became attached to "holy" places, times and objects, to the growing number of sacramentals, even to the veneration of the eucharist.[18] All this undoubtedly allowed many elements of biblical Christianity to flow into the everyday lives of the people, and indeed permeated it with religious ideas. Nevertheless, from quite early in the history of the Church, there were many complaints and warnings about the amount of unchristian and positively pagan superstition that found its way into the Church with these practices. This happened in the Roman Empire, and continued to happen every time new tribes and peoples were converted. The result was a considerable obscuring of the person and work of Christ behind secondary items of the faith or even unchristian views, and a fragmentation of religious life. How little cause there often was to admire the enormously rich and varied popular religious life of Christian antiquity and the Middle Ages is shown by these constantly repeated but ineffectual complaints. Innumerable councils and synods and a regular succession of reform movements, orthodox and heterodox, called for a strengthening and purification of religious life and worship.

The official liturgy, and above all the eucharist, was more securely protected from this fragmentation by its deeper ties with Scripture and the apostolic tradition. It was, however, above all strongly affected by the changed position of the Church in society, a position which had been gradually developing in the third cen-

[18] Cf. A. Franz, *Die Messe im deutschen Mittelalter* (Freiburg/Br., 1902), esp. 3–330; E. Dumoutet, *Le Christ selon la chair et la vie liturgique au Moyen-Age* (Paris, 1932); P. Browe, s.j., *Die Verehrung der Eucharistie im Mittelalter* (Munich, 1933); H. B. Meyer, *Luther und die Messe* (Paderborn, 1965): see the references in the index under *Missbräuche, Misstände*.

tury and consolidated itself after Constantine. The Church was now a political force. Since Theodosius it had been declared the only officially recognized religion, and this brought it an unprecedented flow of members, often only superficially converted. It enjoyed numerous privileges, and its leaders rose to important and fashionable positions. In such a situation the *persona* of the Church in its official worship was inevitably different from what it had been in previous centuries.

From the fourth century onwards, churches grew steadily larger, their liturgies steadily more elaborate, the distance between the clergy and the people steadily greater, and the activity of the peoples correspondingly less. This well-known process led to the Latin clerical liturgy of the Middle Ages, with all its many consequences, and was not interrupted until our own century. Since the principles of communities under a monarchical bishop was firmly maintained, it was hardly possible, and was not felt desirable, to celebrate the liturgy in smaller groups. The ideal was the city community assembled for worship round its bishop, and this ideal continued to be influential even after dioceses had become so big that priests had to represent the bishop at the head of communities. Both in spreading cities and in the country the legally and economically independent parish, which was often, and is still today, of considerable size, replaced the community round the bishop. As at diocesan level, a tendency grew for political boundaries to coincide with ecclesiastical ones. The liturgical and political communities were largely identical, and in a society now Christian there was an automatic and intensive interpenetration. The dedication or patronal feast of the church, the various events and processions in the course of the Church year, the markets or fairs held on such days, liturgical ceremonies for the reception of the ruler, services and processions in times of war or distress or to celebrate a victory: all these were both religious, liturgical events and political and social events in the whole community. Some of them live on in secularized forms into our own times.

In such phenomena, we can see the effects of a development which had already begun before Constantine and still continues today. From the "fraternal community" there developed diocesan or parochial "great communities" which, as in the case of medieval towns, felt themselves to be as much religious or liturgical communities as political units.[19] In some, mainly rural, areas of Germany, the most important figures in public life after the *Bürgermeister* were until quite recently, and sometimes are even today, the *Pfarrherren* or priestly "lords" of the parish. The worship of these larger communities required new forms of celebration adapted to the size and hierarchical structure of the communities. One source of these was the ceremonial of secular dignitaries, and especially of the imperial court, which was itself based on religious ideas. Another was the Old Testament, which was very much in vogue as a result of the opportunities it gave for elaborate worship. Old Testament influence reached a peak at the beginning of the Middle Ages and, apart from the Mass liturgy, influenced particularly the liturgy of ordination and the rites for the anointing and consecration of emperors and kings, which contributed to the religious and political legitimation of the ruler. These rites may be regarded as the positive side of the Church ban, the development of the early Church's discipline of excommunication, which could make or break a political leader.

There are many signs which indicate a clear awareness of the social significance of liturgical acts. The Roman emperors after the third century were not the only ones to invoke the Church's public worship in support of the welfare of the state. The Germanic rulers who inherited the Roman Empire also made efforts to ensure the purity and uniformity of worship in their territories. Charlemagne with his court theologian Alcuin is one example. Liturgical questions were as important a political factor in the mission to the Slavs as centuries later in the time of the Reformation and in both cases the language question was crucial. In post-Renaissance times absolutist rulers and enlightened theologians tried to use public worship as a means of education and an instrument of policy. Nor was it only medieval and earlier rulers who regarded it as important to have their names mentioned in the official liturgy. At the request of the emperor Franz Josef I of Austria, a decree of the Sacred Congregation of Rites dated 10 February 1860 laid down the form in which mention should be made of the emperor in the Mass, in the *Easter Exsultet*

[19] Cf. B. Möller, *Reichsstadt und Reformation* (Gütersloh, 1962), p. 25.

and in the litany of the saints.[20] In the new pagan states of Marxist or fascist origin considerable efforts have been, and still are, made to hinder or suppress worship and replace it with pseudoreligious rites. These include parades, special times for celebration or dedication, secularized forms of veneration of saints and relics —anyone who has visited the Lenin Mausoleum in Moscow will appreciate this—dedicaton ceremonies for young people, secularized marriage and burial rituals.[21]

III. Interpretation and Assessment

There is little room for disagreement about the existence of the facts mentioned in the last section or about their actual importance to the lives of their societies. This is not true of their interpretation and assessment. About this not only Christian but also those who are indifferent or hostile to Christianity may hold different opinions. For this reason we shall end with a few remarks on this aspect.

In this connection the most important point seems to me to be that the New Testament writings, because of restrictions deriving from their situation and period of origin and because of their purpose, contain no specific recommendations for the practice of the Christianity which developed—to use sociological language—from a sect into a universal Church. This process brought with it tasks and problems which never occurred to the New Testament writers.   On its own understanding, the Church was entrusted with a universal mission of salvation, which it tried to carry out by preaching and worship. One consequence of this was that the Church was never just an association to satisfy otherwise unfulfilled personal religious needs, but nevertheless its public status in the Roman Empire was at first merely that of a private religious association, and its liturgy could claim no public character. Christians might, as we have seen, stress loyalty to the constitution and pray for the public good, but, at least in the apostolic age and more generally until into the fourth century, public

[20] On this document see L. Biehl, *Das liturgische Gebet für Kaiser und Reich*, pp. 170–3.
[21] Cf. H.-J. Gamm, *Der braune Kult* (Hamburg, 1962); K. Vondung, *Magie und Manipulation. Ideologischer Kult und politische Religion des Nationalsozialismus* (Göttingen, 1971).

affairs generally, no less than public religion, could not be an active Christian concern.

It was nevertheless Christianity's universal character and absolute claim—almost through the disputes of the persecution period which they provoked—which brought it victory over the pagan state worship. The Christian liturgy thus acquired responsibility for ensuring the peace, safety and welfare of the Empire and justifying its new position as the acknowledged worship of the state. This gave it a publicity it had not previously enjoyed. From this new public status and social significance of the Church and its liturgy followed the exemptions from taxation and civic duties enjoyed by the clergy, the various privileges of Church leaders, the state's acceptance of responsibility for places of worship and their upkeep and its interest in doctrinal and liturgical unity as political factors. Nor was the situation limited to the Roman Empire, but continued into later centuries. The Church settlement of Josef II in Austria is another form of it, and Protestant Church regulations also show how rapidly and completely Reformed liturgies also became official public worship, regulated and authorized by the state.

The Church was largely unprepared for the new responsibilities laid upon it and its liturgy as a result of its transformation into an officially recognized and encouraged religious body.[22] The New Testament, as we have seen, offered little help. There seemed to be essentially two possibilities. The first was to draw on the Old Testament, in particular the Temple liturgy of the pre-exilic period. This and the theology of kingship of the Old Testament, of which the New Testament was regarded from the beginning as the fulfilment, offered the Church, as it were, models from its own pre-history which could help it to meet the new situation. The models were all the more readily adopted as the dispute with Judaism, and the consequent pressure to be different from it, declined in importance. The second possibility was the adoption and attempted christianization of existing social structures, intellectual and linguistic habits and finally religious practices.

[22] On this section see P. Cornehl, "Öffentlicher Gottesdienst. Zum Strukturwandel der Liturgie", in P. Cornehl and H.-E. Bahr (eds.), *Gottesdienst und Öffentlichkeit* (Hamburg, 1970), pp. 118–96, esp. 140–8.

THE SOCIAL SIGNIFICANCE OF THE LITURGY 49

It is not simply understandable, it was also inevitable that the Church should have used both the first and the second of these techniques. Where else could it have got the materials with which to make itself and its message intelligible to the men of these different periods and cultures? And is not the liturgy of its very nature dependent to an unusual degree on the particular customs and forms of celebration of a society and a period? How otherwise could it carry out its task of integrating the whole of public and private life into a single convincing system of meaning, a task carried out in the liturgy through symbolic representation and therefore requiring the use of action, experience and sight?

We have a right, and indeed a duty, to make critics of post-Constantinian Christianity face these questions. We have no need to be frightened of the superior tone in which it is so often alleged that the Church's liturgy has become part of the power structure.[23] Power, after all, and intellectual and spiritual power in particular, is something good so long as it is not artificially distorted and made an end in itself instead of a means—in the case of the liturgy a means to the encounter with God in worship. Even giving stability to secular power, which was a direct or indirect effect of the liturgy, cannot be regarded as automatically bad, unless in particular cases it reinforces unjust authority and delays necessary changes. In addition, a case can be made that while the official liturgy was hierarchically structured, it had no other exclusive distinctions by status, age, sex, and so on, but kept the experience of Christian brotherhood available through the centuries and prepared the ground for necessary social changes. It would be worth while considering this point in more detail.

It must certainly be firmly accepted that criticism of the actual history of the liturgy is justified to the extent that a great variety of mistakes has been made in all periods, and these should not be minimized. The attempt to assimilate Old Testament and pagan religious practices has led repeatedly, usually in combination with parallel tendencies in the history of theology and religious politics, to serious distortions of the Christian liturgy. In the East

[23] Cf. P. Cornehl, "Öffentlicher Gottesdienst", pp. 147–8.

there has been a tendency to build the official liturgy into an overwhelming mystery play, the terrifying scope of which can be made known only to God's consecrated ministers. In the West, through the influence of sacralizing and legalistic tendencies, there developed a clerical liturgy in which the people were reverent spectators but understood, and did, less and less. Moreover, the liturgy is everywhere threatened by magical interpretations, above all in popular devotions and practices. Nor can it be denied that the "stewards of the mysteries of God" did not always express the power they enjoyed in Christian societies in the form of self-denying service. The dangers of service turning into domination, of sacramental authority used to obtain political and social power and of attempts by secular authorities to make use of the Church's spiritual power for their own ends led in the past to many tensions between clergy and people and between ecclesiastical and secular authorities. This danger will continue to exist as long as the Church, in its liturgy and its preaching, makes a claim to public status and authority, a claim from which, however, it can no longer retreat, in spite of the possibility it involves of false interpretations and wrong developments.

It is hardly possible to say today whether, and how, these false developments could have been avoided, but it is certainly possible to claim that the liturgy can be shown to have had, and to have still, considerable social effect. We have looked at some of the evidence. More evidence comes from the actions of those who take a critical view of the past developments or try today to restrict or stifle worship. Even today, however, warnings against direct attempts to use worship for political and social ends are still necessary.[24] A tool used for the wrong purpose becomes blunt and ineffective. The celebration of the liturgy has a variety of effects in the life of the individual believer and of the community of the Church. It creates stability, gives meaning, induces repentance and inspires action. For each of these, however, it must first be taken seriously in its fundamental aspect, that of an encounter with God mediated by signs.

Translated by Francis McDonagh

[24] On this see H. B. Meyer, *Politik im Gottesdienst?*

John Navone

Evil and its Symbols

THE Devil has been the classic symbol of evil for the people of God; however, he has been depicted quite differently. Early Greek Christians depicted the Devil as a handsome, charming young man. They recognized that evil is so attractive and power-fully seductive that men cede or consent to its temptation. The appropriate symbol for evil had to be personal and appealing; it had to be apparently good. The art of the Middle Ages, however, portrayed the Devil as an ugly and horrifying monster. Its symbol of evil stressed the effects rather than the cause of evil. The medieval Devil symbolized personal evil which alters and deforms the natural, corporeal and spiritual integrity of man. Guilt, moral pain, psychoses and neuroses deprive the spirit of man of its natural equilibrium and integrity; hence, it is appropriately sym-bolized by a personal, deformed, quasi-bestial or less-than-human, figure. In morality plays, the Devil was presented as the deceiver of men and adversary of Christ; he could always be recognized, despite his disguise, by the limp which resulted from his fall from heaven.

Other symbolic representations of evil reveal its nature as a blemish, stain, or impurity, and through a progressive interior-ization of evil, as transgression, deviation, or sin and finally, as burden or charge weighing on conscience (culpability, guilt). The symbolization of evil develops from the magical to the ethical. Evil, first conceived as a quality of action, comes to qualify the agent himself as evil or culpable. The symbols of stain, deviation and burden attempt to represent the nature of evil; for Christians, they are associated with the mystery of iniquity which envelops mankind. Inasmuch as moral evils hinge upon human performance for their existence, they are often symbolized by the Devil, devils and other personal beings.

The current outcropping of Satanism and the wave of interest with the occult in both film and novels ("The Devils", "The Exorcist", "Rosemary's Baby", "The Possession of Joel Delaney", "The Other", "The Mefisto Waltz", "The Damned", etc.) as well as in popular cult, point to a culture which has lost its balance in a flood of symbols for evil. The Devil and kindred malignant spirits seem to be of perennial interest, although this interest is often enough not of a serious or religious nature. The fascination for the demonic, witchcraft and the occult has happened before. Out of the rationalism of the Enlightenment sprang the witch trials, out of the heart of scholasticism alchemy. There seems to be a personal and collective unconscious which demands the creation of symbols of evil, and which is served by them. Foreign devils, for example, in one form or another symbolize a threat to the integrity and existence of every society.

II. FOREIGN DEVILS

Foreigners, as well as people of a different race or culture, are generally regarded with suspicion. They easily become symbols of evil because they are alien; their radical difference is felt as a threat to existence and values of the *status quo*. The Chinese spoke of "foreign devils" and many other cultures have shared similar sentiments about foreigners.

The Anglo-Saxon world's literature and drama is rich in "foreign devils", among which the Italians have been perhaps the most common. The religious antagonism of the Reformation is largely responsible. On the other hand, the Italian "devils" reveal the traditional way in which the Anglo-Saxon world thinks of Mediterranean man in particular and of swarthy people in general. Darkness, danger and mystery are closely related concepts in the Anglo-Saxon's symbolization of evil. (The American Blacks' slogan, "black is beautiful", is meant to offset this prejudice.)

The Italian "foreign devils" had their roots in a land sufficiently within English consciousness to become an object for reflection; yet, sufficiently alien so as to remain somewhat beyond comprehension. Italy was a known unknown, at once familiar and mysterious, proximate and elusive, sunlit and obscure.

The exotic and mysterious presence of Italy was strongly felt in the Elizabethan and Jacobean theatre where Italy was considered the academy of manslaughter, the sporting place of murder, the apothecary shop of all nations. English playwrights of the period comfortably assume that the land of the pope and of Machiavelli is the home of vice and crime. John Webster, John Ford, Thomas Middleton and Cyril Tourneur, spellbound by the myth of Italian wickedness, thrilled English crowds with their Italian "foreign devils".

Machiavelli was the symbol of the Devil incarnate for most Elizabethans. His books were considered the grammar of a diabolical creed, of materialism tinged with satanism. His motive for writing *The Prince* was missed: the vision of a liberated Italy, redeemed by the one thing that could unite it, the dominance of a just, firm, efficient leader. Unlike Italy, England was not a country occupied by foreigners, given over to civil conflict for which there seemed no remedy in the ordinary course of political events.

Gothic novels of the eighteenth century were filled with Italian "devils". There was Walpole's Manfred, Radcliffe's Schedoni and Montoni, Lewis' Coelestino and Flodoardo, Mary Shelley's Castruccio, Maturin's Schemoli and Morosini, Landor's Fra Rupert, and Moore's Zeluco. The criminal monk type was the most common of the foreign devils. These preternaturally malevolent monks were endowed with the qualities of a super-humanity; they inflicted grievous harm on innocent victims. There were also satanic tyrant types, sublime criminals, motivated by joy in malevolence, lust and the thirst for power. These foreign devils move in the demonic underworld of caverns and dungeons, amid labyrinthine vaults and corridors, in which so much of the evil occurs. They move in a world which has its roots in the mythic subconscious strata of our lives, the levels we now call archetypal. They symbolize those evils threatening what is English, open, clear, moral and Protestant; they are malevolent dark people menacing wholesome light people. They endanger the cherished value system.

The recent spate of Mafia books and the success of *The Godfather* in the United States suggests that the Italian variety of foreign devil is still very much in fashion in the English-speaking world, and that it is not entirely the product of Anglo-Saxon racism, religious bigotry and imagination. When the Italian genius for organization is perverted, there are elements for Gothic tales of terror in any epoch. Imperialism, capitalism, clerical *romanità*, fascism and Mafia connote large segments of human activity in which the fine Italian hand has, at one time or another, exerted a sinister influence upon millions. The Italian foreign devils gave the West its first prolonged experience of imperialism. They helped religion run awry in the vagaries of clerical *romanità* and overcentralization. They promoted the usurious practices of Europe's first capitalists, bankers and bookkeepers. Machiavellian and fascist politics, as well as Mafia crime, are among their most distinctive specialties. Hence, the English-speaking world's Italian foreign devils imply the rejection of the authentic evils which they symbolize, as well as the recognition that the excellence of human life in any society requires that it be exorcized of its devils, native and foreign, English or American, and Italian.

Societies must recognize the foreign devils within their politics, business and social life, religion and crime, before they can effectively exorcize them. Their creation of symbols for them is a first step in the process of exorcism. The evils must be named, described and symbolized before a society can exorcize them; a vague sense of their presence is insufficient for the task. On the other hand, exorcism has its risks. The Devil is a liar. He may succeed in withholding his true name and in imputing his evil to the innocent. The exorcist must be a holy man; otherwise, he may be deceived and destroyed by the very devils he attempts to exorcize. Recent history bears witness to the catastrophic results produced by unholy men attempting to exorcize their societies of its foreign devils.

Why should the devils afflicting society be envisioned as foreign? Perhaps such a symbolization of evil provides that vicarious experience of innocence which may be conducive to the

attainment of a genuine personal and social wholeness. It is necessary to be able to imagine a society free of the (d)evils that beset
it before it is possible to exorcize it from those (d)evils. Imagining
them as foreign (d)evils is one step in the process of alienating
them. They are, in fact, foreign to the natural good of both the
individual and society; hence, they can be envisioned as foreigners
besieging them from without, as aliens who do not belong.

The symbolization of evil in terms of foreign devils may also
be a facile way of shirking responsibility for those evils threatening the integrity of the community by placing the blame for
them on others. In times of national crisis, Chinese, Indian and
Jewish merchants have been regarded as the foreign devils of
Asian, African and Western nations; and, as in an exorcism, they
have been expelled for the imagined good of the community.
Evils besetting the Catholic community have been symbolized by
both Roman and Dutch foreign devils. The Reformation might
be viewed as an attempt to exorcize the Christian community of
its Roman devil. Today, there are those who would like to exorcize the Church of its Dutch devil; however, a heightened awareness of theological and moral complexity precludes the easy
exorcisms of past times. This new awareness has also rendered
the symbolization of evil considerably more difficult. The devils
have to be identified, or clearly symbolized, before the process of
exorcism can get under way. Furthermore, there may be a greater
reluctance to cast our devils into the outer darkness among those
who may, after all, be "anonymous Christians". The line between
the people of God and the Gentiles, pagans, infidels and heretics
is no longer so sharply drawn as in the days when most of the
Church's enemies were envisioned as those outside it. Such devils
were authentically foreign. Today, evils within the Church, elements foreign to the spirit of Christ, may still qualify for symbolization as "foreign" devils; they are "spirits" contrary to that
of Christ, rather than nations or races.

III. The Wilderness Symbol of Evil

Wilderness has long been a symbol of evil. Even modern
authors discuss slum conditions and urban degeneracy under

such titles as *The City Wilderness*[1] and *The Neon Wilderness*.[2]
A study of metropolitan areas refers to "this new 'wilderness'
that has grown up in Magalopolis".[3] The implication is that
modern man feels as insecure and confused in an urban setting
as he once felt in the forest among wild beasts and the frightening
creatures of his imagination.[4]

Wilderness is the environment of the non-human and even anti-
human, the place of wild beasts, where the control and order
which man imposes on the natural world is absent and where
man is an alien presence.[5] Wilderness refers to the unruly, confused, disordered world of creatures not under the control of
man. In the Old English of the eighth-century epic *Beowulf*, the
term (wildēor) refers to savage and fantastic beasts inhabiting a
dismal region of forests and cliffs.

Wilderness as the habitat of wild beasts implied the absence of
men and a region where a person was likely to get into a disordered, confused or "wild" condition. The semi-human Wild
Man, for example, was the most important imaginary denizen of
the wildernesses of medieval Europe. He appeared widely in the
art, literature and drama of the period. He lived in the heart of

---

[1] R. Woods (Boston, 1898). The theatre of the absurd gives eloquent
expression to man's experience of the wilderness condition: Albee, Adamov,
Arrabal, Beckett, Genet, Ionesco. The existentialists Sartre and Camus do
the same.

[2] N. Algren (New York, 1960). Arthur Miller's *Death of a Salesman* em-
ploys considerable wilderness imagery to express the perils of life in modern
society.

[3] J. Gottmann, *Megalopolis* (New York, 1961), p. 216.

[4] Lucretius spoke for his age in *De Rerum Natura* when he observed that
it was a serious defect that so much of the earth was possessed of wilderness full of restless dread. He describes this as the context of precivilized
life, where man lived a nightmarish existence, hounded by dangers on all
sides. He relates how man escaped his miserable wilderness condition
through the development of his intelligence and inventions.

[5] There were other elements basic to man's hostility and terror of the
wilderness. Many folk traditions associate the wilderness with the supernatural and monstrous. It had a quality of mystery that triggered the
imagination. To frightened eyes the limbs of trees became grotesque, leap-
ing figures, and the wind sounded like a weird scream. The wild forest
seemed animated with fantastic creatures lurking in its depths. Whether
propitiated with sacrifices as deities or regarded as devils, these forest beings
were feared. See A. Porteus, *Forest Folklore, Mythology, and Romance*
(New York, 1928).

the forest as far as possible from civilization. He symbolized what happened to the isolated man of the wilderness, living outside the human community, alienated from God and man. He was a savage ogre who devoured children and ravished maidens.[6] Alienation made him a monster.

Man is "bewildered" in an alien environment where the civilization that normally orders and controls his life is absent. Such an environment produces a state of mind in which man feels lost, stripped of guidance, perplexed, and at the mercy of alien, mysterious and malign forces. This concept has extended the meaning of the word to include large and disordered collections of things, even if man-made.

Among most early cultures, paradise was man's greatest good; wilderness, as its antipode, was his greatest evil. In one condition the environment, garden-like, ministered to his every desire. ("Eden" was the Hebrew word for "delight".) In the other condition it was frequently dangerous, and always beyond control. For primitive man existence in the wilderness was precarious. Safety, happiness and progress all seemed dependent on rising out of a wilderness situation. Human development was synonymous with man's gaining control over nature. Fire, the domestication of some wild animals, and the raising of crops were gradual steps. The reduction of the wilderness area measured man's advance towards civilization.

The Hebrews hated and feared the wilderness as a cursed land because of its forbidding character and lack of water.[7] Men could not survive for long in such an inhospitable environment. When their God wished to threaten or punish a sinful people, he found the wilderness condition to be his most powerful weapon: "I will lay waste the mountains and hills, and dry up all their herbage" (Deut. 8. 15). Sodom and Gomorrah became parched wastes and thorny bush as a penalty for the sins of their citizens.

[6] Pan, lord of the woods in classical mythology, had the legs, ears and tail of a goat and the body of a man. He combined gross sensuality with boundless energy. Greeks passing through forests dreaded an encounter with Pan. The word "panic" originated from the blinding fear that seized travellers upon hearing strange cries in the wilderness and assuming them to signify Pan's approach.

[7] R. Funk, "The Wilderness", *Journal of Biblical Literature*, 78 (1959), pp. 205–14.

The identification of the arid wasteland with God's curse led to the belief that the wilderness was the environment of evil, a kind of hell populated by malign spirits. Among them were the howling dragon or *tan*, the winged female monster of the night called the *Lilith*, and the familiar man-goat, *Seirim*. Presiding over all was *Azazel*, the arch-devil of the wilderness. In an expiatory rite the chief priest of a community symbolically laid the sins of the group upon a goat and sent it away into the wilderness to Azazel (Deut. 16. 10). The ritual of the scapegoat reveals the Hebrew view of the wilderness.

The Old Testament treatment of the paradise theme conveys this idea of the immorality of wild country. Eden was a place without fear, the antipode of the wilderness; the creatures that lived there were peaceful and helpful. As a punishment for eating the forbidden fruit Adam and Eve were driven out of the Garden into the wilderness, a "cursed" land full of "thorns and thistles". The author of Joel juxtaposes Eden and the wilderness: "The land is like the garden of Eden before them, but after them a desolate wilderness" (2. 3). And Isaiah communicates the promise that God will comfort Zion and "make her wilderness like Eden, her desert like the garden of the Lord" (51. 3). The wilderness and paradise are both physical and spiritual opposites.

Wilderness, for Christians, has long been a powerful symbol applied either to the moral chaos of the unregenerate or to the godly man's conception of life on earth as a pilgrim in an alien land struggling against temptations endangering his spiritual life. Wilderness symbolizes the human condition as a compound of the natural inclination to sin, the temptation of the material world, and the forces of evil themselves. In his wilderness experience of the world, the flesh and the devil, the Christian looks to Christ and his community for deliverance. Community symbolizes salvation; wilderness symbolizes perdition. The Christian is supported by Christ and his community in his struggle for survival against the evils of the wilderness. He envisages his salvation in terms of the community, Kingdom, Church of Christ, the antipode of the moral and spiritual wilderness of the lost.

Jesus forms his community to save man from the wilderness, only after he had himself undergone the trials of the wilderness experience.[8] His forty days in the wilderness (= desert) recalls the forty years of temptation and tribulation which Israel had undergone in the wilderness of Sinai. "Full of the Holy Spirit" (Lk. 4. 1), Jesus enters the wilderness, the natural habitat of those evil spirits which trouble men and throw them into confusion. The Hebraic folk imagination, like that of other cultures, made the wilderness the abode of demons and devils.

In his wilderness experience Jesus confronts the malign forces which beset all mankind. He experiences a genuine period of trial and suffering, a real, interior experience, more profoundly significant than the more externalized, literal interpretation in which he would actually have been taken up to the Temple pinnacle. It is an experience which, according to St Luke, is intimately linked with Jesus' death. After the temptations, the Devil departs from Jesus "for a while" (4. 13), until "the hour" of his death. Satan returns for the death of Jesus: "Satan entered into Judas" (22. 3); and, when Jesus is apprehended at Gethsemane (22. 53), he declares, "This is your hour and the power of darkness". The insistent demands of Satan for a sign, which begin in the temptations of the wilderness, continue to the end of Jesus' life with the mocking cry, "If you are the King of the Jews, save yourself!" (23. 37). The cry echoes Satan's words in the wilderness, "If you are the Son of God..." (4. 3, 9).

There is a second "echo" element in the confusion of Jesus' wilderness trial. The experience is a sequel to his baptism in which he had heard the heavenly voice saying, "You are my beloved Son". In the confusion of the wilderness, Jesus now hears another voice saying, "If you are the Son of God...", and he must discern whether it comes from the same source. Three times Jesus concludes that the voice which prompts him to action is that of Satan. He adheres to the recognition of his unique vocation in his baptismal experience and rejects all unworthy interpretations of it. He comes to a realization, for example, that he should not employ political power for the achievement of his mission. Spiritual discernment, in the face of the bewildering complexity and variety of options confronting man, is a trial from which no man is exempt.

[8] J. Navone, *Themes of St Luke* (Rome, 1970), pp. 170–9.

Christ represents man's triumph over the evils symbolized by the wilderness through his submission to the basic human experience of the wilderness in his historical trial of having to discern God's will for him. Christ's ultimate accomplishment hinged upon his ability to resolve the problems of his historical mission within the given limitations of his human nature and in the face of the confusing complexity and variety of options confronting him. He did not make himself Messiah, nevertheless he had to come to the recognition of his messianic role through the normal process of human experience, understanding, reasoning, judgment and decision. The process of coming to recognize his God-given, historical identity and mission may well have been a type of severe interior trial somewhat comparable to that of all men in quest of their historical identity, meaning and mission.

Jesus has overcome the evils of the wilderness condition in which man feels lost and alien in a hostile world. All men are able to stand in the relationship of children to God precisely through the human nature assumed by Christ (Heb. 2. 14–18). Jesus is the way of the Lord through the human wilderness condition. Not only does he know the way through the wilderness, but he is the exemplar of it and manifests it in his own person. He does not merely proclaim the way, but it is inseparably connected with his person, and it is in his person that the way of God through the wilderness has appeared in the world (Jn. 14. 6). Jesus is the way to communion with God and neighbour; he is the way which re-establishes that community between God and man and among men, overcoming the wilderness condition of alienation, fear, confusion and hostility. Because Jesus *is* the communion of God and man, union with him enables mankind to experience the same reality, the reality which is the way through the wilderness chaos to the Christian cosmos.[9]

The wilderness symbolizes the context in which Jesus and his mission have their meaning. It symbolizes the human condition for which his Church, as an expression of the divine mercy, was instituted to serve as a way of liberation. Mankind's universal ex-

[9] Almost everywhere the expulsion of demons, diseases and sins coincides, or at one period coincided, with the festival of the New Year, celebrating the resumption of time from the beginning in a passage from chaos to cosmos. Such exorcisms effect a kind of new creation.

perience of the wilderness is the only context in which Jesus, his mission and his Church make sense. It symbolizes the experiences which Jesus knew and mastered in his own historical existence, an achievement in which all mankind participates. The personal character of the experience has been symbolized by the Devil and demons which Jesus and his disciples exorcize for the liberation of mankind. Human freedom does not come without the trials of a spiritual struggle in which man must be aided by the liberating power of the Way through the demon-infested wilderness of his own spirit and society (e.g., The Asphalt Jungle, the Blackboard Jungle).

IV. SYMBOLIZATION OF EVIL: PURPOSE, FRUITS, DANGERS

Symbols suggest something else by reason of relationship, association and convention. They are visible signs of what may be invisible, as an idea and attitude. They express an attitude, stance, orientation, feeling. They are what they mean, and mean what they are designated to mean. They may therefore be transformed by the power of a new meaning. Christ, for example, has transformed the meaning of death and the cross into a symbol of salvation; he has transformed the meaning of marriage by designating it as the symbol of his union with the Church (Ephesians 5). Christian marriage is different from non-Christian marriage because its meaning is different. The sacraments are what the sacraments mean, and they mean what Christ instituted them to mean.[10] As symbols of salvation they imply counter-symbols of perdition. Our understanding of grace and evil and their presence to us in and through symbols gives the basis for the social or communal character of worship.[11]

Man is a related being who naturally expresses his relatedness through symbols. He expresses his reactions to the evils which he

[10] F. Crowe, "Salvation as Wholeness", in *Canadian Journal of Theology* 14 (1968), p. 234.
[11] Speculative theology and philosophic efforts to reach God are not immediately relevant to the stimulation of religious feeling, but if one's knowledge of God's existence and one's imperfect understanding of one's faith are to be operative in spontaneity they must be linked with symbols that engage one's sensitivity. Prayer is just such a symbol. It is a sensitive engagement of the psyche associated with one's knowledge and belief.

experiences in nature, in himself, and in society through symbols which imply his apprehension of values. His symbols of evil express his feelings of fear or aversion, and they also evoke these feelings. They have the power of expressing what man may be unable to express in a more logical and refined way; nevertheless, they complement a logical explanation by meeting a need which it cannot meet. This is the need for an affective response to the objects of his awareness.[12]

Symbols do not explain themselves; they need critical examination because they are open to multiple meanings.[13] Symbols of liberation for some are symbols of oppression for others. The explanation of the symbol goes beyond the symbol; it is necessary for the intelligent and effective use of the symbol for social action or communal worship.[14] The exorcist must know the name of (understand) the devil (the symbolized evil) before he can exorcize it; knowledge is essential for effective remedies for the evils besetting man. An erroneous understanding of the evils symbolized may lead a community to ineffectual, stupid, or even disastrous action. *Mein Kampf*, for example, provides non-economic symbols for economic ills. There is also the tendency to make the symbol the explanation for evils, as a panacea in reverse. Communism, fascism, the Vietnam war, the middle class, drugs, the Church, and so on, become symbols for everything that is wrong in society.

Antithesis is an important means of persuasion, as when a policy is recommended in terms of what it is against. There is a constant temptation of societies to achieve purgation by scapegoat, congregation by segregation. In the polemics of politics, the use of the scapegoat to establish identification in terms of an enemy

[12] B. Lonergan, *Method in Theology* (London, 1971), pp. 64–9.

[13] P. Ricoeur, *The Symbolism of Evil* (Boston, 1967), p. 351. Through critical interpretation, aided by the insights of all the sciences, religious symbols regain their power to transmit the sacred. We must understand to believe, and we must believe to understand fully.

[14] E. Erikson, "The Development of Ritualisation", in *The World Year Book of Religion*, I (London, 1969), p. 712, maintains that ritualization is essential for human development: separateness transcended and distinctiveness confirmed in the mutuality of recognition. The wilderness condition is dehumanizing for its lack of authentic community with God and man; it is devoid of that ritualization which characterizes authentically human relationships with God and man.

shared in common enables the candidate who presents himself as spokesman for the community to prod his audience to consider local ills primarily in terms of alien figures ("foreign devils") viewed as the outstanding causes of those ills. The symbols of evil must be used wisely; otherwise, they may bring upon their users the very evils they symbolize.

V. Man as Symbol

Man is a symbol, the *imago Dei*.[15] His actions express and are the very meaning of his life. The good man reflects the glory of God as a visible manifestation of God's invisible nature (Rom. I. 20); the good Christian expresses the glory of God in Christ. The same is true for the good secular society and the good society of Christians. Through evil actions, however, the symbol is perverted; it becomes, according to the measure of evil, a counter-symbol. The evil individual and society misrepresent, distort and falsify the glory of God; the evil Christian individual and community misrepresent, distort and falsify the glory of God in Christ. As symbols of evil, they tend to mislead men in quest of God in Christ. As symbols of evil, they tend to mislead men in quest of God and his perfect Image in Christ; they tend to corrupt the human understanding of God and his perfect expression in his Word. Perhaps the only evils which New Testament account reveals as provoking the anger of Christ are those misrepresentations of God and his spirit by the official religious leaders. They had, in many respects, become counter-symbols of that God for whom Jesus was the perfect symbol. They tended to falsify the very reality which Jesus verified through his personal communication of the experience, knowledge, love and understanding of God.

The mutual love of Christians is the efficacious symbol which communicates Christ to others: "By this all men will know that you are my disciples, if you have love for one another (Jn. 13. 35). Hatred and strife among Christians is the correlative counter-symbol which misrepresents, distorts and falsifies Christ for others. Hatred among Christians is the supreme symbol of evil

---

[15] See R. Rousseau, "Secular and Christian Images of Man", in *Thought* 47 (1972), pp. 167–200.

because it deprives others of the authentic revelation of God's love in Christ; because it is the culpable failure to communicate the divine mercy for the fulfilment of others; because it tends to render the meaning of God in Christ contemptible for others. The ecumenical imperative for Christians derives from their commitment to that mutual love, corresponding to that of Christ and his Father (Jn. 15. 9 f.), which reveals God in Christ to mankind. Ecumenical prayer services and friendly collaboration among the many Christian denominations enable Christians to become effective symbols of mutual love rather than symbols of evil.

Joan Llopis

The Message of Liberation in the Liturgy

BEFORE making any comment on the relationship between liturgy and politics, we have to analyse the meaning of the proclamation of the word within the celebration of the liturgy. This does not imply any neglect of ritual and symbol, and certainly does not involve any view of the liturgy as mere verbal activity. It is none the less true that the importance of the word in the liturgy must be stressed, and especially the qualitative value of words in their liturgical context. My aim in this article is to analyse the relationship between the words of the liturgy and the *political dimension* in the faith and life of the Christian community.

I. THE LITURGY PROCLAIMS A MESSAGE OF LIBERATION

Within the actions of the liturgy, there are many kinds of words: biblical readings, prayers, hymns, admonitions and homilies. Each has its own texture and its own dynamic, but all try to express the sole reality that the Christian community can express with meaning: the good news of salvation. The tone and approach may be different, there are various literary genres involved, but the content of the message is the same: Jesus is salvation. The three principal kinds of liturgical statement found in the eucharistic celebration can be reduced to three brief sentences which differ only in their grammatical subject. Proclaiming the word, God himself says "*I* am the Saviour". In the profession of faith, the believing community affirms: "*He* is the Saviour", and

65

finally the anaphora brings all together in a loving dialogue with the Lord: "*You* are the Saviour".[1]

Salvation, as proclaimed in the liturgy through the word, is not a disembodied, purely supernatural reality. It is specifically Christian, and therefore part of the web of human history. Theology today puts great emphasis on the relationship between the two concepts of salvation and liberation. The latter is understood in the widest possible sense.[2] The message conveyed in the liturgy, if it is to be Christian, must be one of liberation.

There is nothing arbitrary in the view that salvation and liberation are equivalent terms—in fact this accords with biblical revelation. In the Old Testament, the historical experience of the exodus provides a key to the inner meaning of salvation. In the words of Moses to the people (cf. Ex. 13. 3–4) it is possible to interpret the fact of the exodus of the people from Egypt at three different levels. First, there is the basic historical fact: the people move out, just as any other nomad group might, and the record of the move is found in the chronicles of the historians. At the second level there is the political interpretation of the historical fact—the exodus is seen as a movement from slavery to freedom, a process of liberation set in a political context. At the final level, the religious interpretation of the event is advanced. The deepest meaning of the departure of Israel is found in the divine intervention, with God as the chief protagonist. That is to say, we can go from a verifiable historical datum (the migrations) to a political dimension (liberation) and so to a deeper level, that of its religious meaning (divine salvation). The human experience of going forth and winning freedom both realizes and makes manifest a salvation whose subject is God himself.

It must be emphasized that these three levels are not to be considered as separate and juxtaposed, but that there is a profound unity between the religious level and the historical and political level. The first shows the most meaningful aspect of all human liberation, and so the exodus stands as a paradigm for all Jewish

[1] A. Manaranche, *Je crois en Jésus-Christ aujourd'hui* (Paris, 1968), p. 36.

[2] G. Gutiérrez, *Teología de la liberación* (Salamanca, 1972); R. A. Alves, *Cristianismo ¿opio o liberación?* (Salamanca, 1973); *A Theology of Human Hope* (Washington, 1969); J. Alfaro, *Esperanza cristiana y liberación del hombre* (Barcelona, 1972).

and Christian religious experience.[3] Yahweh is to be seen in history, if history is read with the eyes of faith, which alone can change the subject of history. The going forth of the Israelites is the going forth of God, the liberation of the people is the salvation of God and the history of the world is God's own salvation history.

In the New Testament, the vision of the Old reaches its culminating point. The paradigm of the exodus finds its perfect fulfilment in the work of Christ, put forward by the New Testament as liberation. His death and resurrection are particularly seen as the true, definitive exodus (cf. Lk. 9. 31: Jn. 13. 1). The paschal mystery of Jesus Christ, the central object of preaching and the liturgy, in this way becomes a mystery of liberation. It fulfils all the prefigurations of the Old Testament and stands as a guarantee of the eschatological future.

The paschal liberation of Christ, though superseding the exodus, is linked to that earlier liberation. Christian salvation is founded and is incarnate in the human reality of liberation, but no attempt to translate it into concrete reality can ever be regarded as final or definitive. It follows that all instances of liberation must be scrutinized with a critical eye. This tension between incarnation and criticism generates the prophetic dimension of the Christian message, with its need to create new movements of liberation which anticipate in time eschatological salvation. Hence Christian salvation is incarnate in the work of human liberation. It is the touchstone for any historical, practical form this may take. It also becomes the prophetic promise of definitive liberty.[4]

II. The Message without Liberation

We have affirmed that the liturgy proclaims the message of liberation. To be more exact, however, the liturgy is meant to do this, but often does not. Certain conditions are required for the message of the liturgy to be truly grasped and lived in its full liberating force. To understand clearly what these conditions are, it may be best to glance first at the circumstances which prevent

[3] D. Daube, *The Exodus Pattern in the Bible* (London, 1963).
[4] S. Pie, "¿Què és la salvación?", *De la fe a la teología* (Barcelona, 1973), pp. 3–20.

this from happening. Christian salvation derives its character as human liberation from its insertion into history, since history is the special ambit of liberty. The greatest obstacle to a truly liberating proclamation of the word in the liturgy must therefore be the failure to incarnate this in historical time. This failure may relate to the past, the present or the future.

In the case of the past, the word loses its historical dimension when it is proclaimed in a mythical form. The myth narrates events which are outside the framework of history because they are set in a time outside time itself. In mythical narratives, we cannot really speak of an historical past, but only of an archetypal time ever recurring and ever unchanging. To connect the present with mythical time prevents man from being truly free, since his destiny is to some extent preordained in the unchanging character of the events put before us as our exemplar. The liturgical proclamation of the word constantly risks being confused with the narration of eternal, unchanging myths, and risks the consequent loss of that insertion into history which it must have. Several factors contribute to this—the ritual elements which accompany the proclamation, the cyclic repetition of the same texts throughout the feasts of the liturgical year and the undeniably mythical aspects of certain stories in the Bible. When the word is stifled by the myth, it loses its power to free men. It enslaves the present and future of man to the tyranny of a timeless, inhuman past.

In the present, the word loses its historical dimension when it is proclaimed in an ideological form. Every ideology claims to stand as an absolute system of values which requires acceptance for its own sake, without taking into account the concrete circumstances of the present moment. Although anxious to be related to the present, it does not consider the present in its historical aspect as such, but only as one link in a chain, no different from any of the others. An ideology believes that it possesses eternal truth, and the present only concerns it to the extent that it enables immutable ideas to be actualized. All this leads to a lack of historical perspective, and the consequent destruction of man's free action in the quest for the ideological model, designed to be valid for all circumstances. The risk frequently threatening the liturgical word is that it will degenerate into an ideology and become cut off from what is happening now in history. The doctrinal weight of many biblical texts contributes to this and so does the theological explanation which accompanies them, especially through the homily. It is only too easy to forget the primary kerygmatic value of the word, and give a one-sided doctrinal, or doctrinaire, view of the texts concerned. When the word is dominated by ideology, it isolates the present from its historical past and eschatological future, and fetters it to inflexible "eternal truths".

In relation to the future, the word loses its historical dimension when it is proclaimed in utopian fashion, that is, when it looks to a future fulfilment which we know in advance cannot be achieved. This kind of utopianism denies the historical future, even though it appears to offer a futurist vision. Its future lies outside time, in isolation from the real history of men. Utopian aspirations destroy liberty, since man is condemned by them to aspire all the time towards a goal he cannot reach, beyond his real possibilities. The word proclaimed in the liturgy can easily be made to sound like a utopian promise. Its eschatological aspect, its burden of hope, its advocacy of a kind of superhuman ideal can all contribute to the belief that the gospel message is utopian, even chimerical. The confusion between eschatological promise and utopian ideal can have an enslaving effect on the hearer of the word, since it can discourage him in his struggle to free himself from the weight of evil and sin. When the word preaches Utopia, the danger is that the reality of man's past and present will be sacrificed on the altar of an all-consuming, impossible future.

III. The Message of Liberty

If the liturgical proclamation of the word is to lose none of its power to free man, it must maintain contact with history and make a real impact on the past, present and future. This means that myth must be opposed by memory, ideology by interpellation and Utopia by promise.

To proclaim the word as memory, as the remembrance of the past, implies a conviction that the deeds which the gospel message refers to belong to the real history of men. They are not mythical incidents lost in the darkness of time, nor are they pious anecdotes or little moral tales. On the contrary, they are always fully human events with all the social and political factors involved which belong to the real life of men. Seen in the light of faith, these happenings demonstrate the liberating intervention of God in world history, and thereby deserve to be kept green in the memory of the Church. This is not the same as being preserved in historical archives, like desiccated records of the past. The memory of the Church is a vivid, present-day enactment of the deeds remembered, because the liberating force that made them possible continues to operate now. The same Spirit that led the people of Israel from slavery to freedom, and led the Jews from death to life, now sustains the faith of the community listening to the proclamation of the wonders of the Lord. To the extent that this faith has as its object decisive events in the history of human liberation, the word-memory which actualizes them is potentially a force for freedom in the Church and in the world.

To proclaim the word as an interpellation, a demand for an explanation, implies belief in the validity of the message for today. It does not mean that the biblical message contains a perfectly thought-out ideology which will fit all times and all situations. The message in fact refers to events in the historical past, but the present for salvation and liberation can only emerge from the past. The believing community knows that what the Lord of history did in favour of our fathers in the past, he can continue to do in our favour through present-day instances of liberation. The word, when it is proclaimed, speaks of the past and gives us light for the present. The present is not a copy of the past, because it always entails new and original elements which allow us to discover a new wealth of meaning in the ancient words. The liturgical proclamation of the word can and must impinge on present-day events which affect the process of liberation for men. Reading the "signs of the times", the word acts as a critical interpellation searching out the inadequacy of human achievement but giving fresh impulse all the time to new and better efforts. The effect on the Church and the world is to counteract any temptation to either complacency or discouragement.

To proclaim the word as promise means that its efficacy for the real future of history is emphasized. It is not limited to past deeds or to the transitory present. It announces the definitive consummation of history, not as something apart, detached from the past and the present, but rather as a dimension underlying the various ways in which the word has been actualized in the past and present. The eschatological promise of the evangelical message does not refer to some utopian, unattainable future—it refers to something which we can achieve now, and which has in fact been realized in the past but is always imperfect, unfinished and therefore in need of constant improvement. The necessary force for this is already present in the world, even if it is never made manifest in all its perfection. Total liberation is present in hope, the hope that liberates mankind in depth by destroying all that could tie him to the illusion that he has reached the end when he is still on the journey. The prophetic proclamation of the word-promise is the greatest guarantee of liberty.

IV. THE DECISIVE ROLE OF THE HOMILY

Memory, interpellation and promise, these three features apply to every single kind of liturgical word. Otherwise these words would lose their liberating force and capacity to make an impact on the political dimension of faith. One special type of word has a particular role in the task of conveying the dynamic, liberating power of the evangelical message. I refer to the homily. Its importance lies in its function as an integrating element for a number of aspects of the liturgy which, without it, would run the risk of dispersion and even disintegration.

This integration occurs at various levels. In the first place, the homily is the hinge for the two integral parts of any celebration—the word and the rite. It unifies not just in an objective fashion, but through its close relationship with the members of the assembly, those who listen to the word and those who celebrate the rite. Secondly, the homily combines the chief characteristics of the other kinds of preaching which exist in the Church. Essentially, it exhorts the hearers to actualize the word through the celebration and through their lives; but it must also preserve the challenge of the missionary message and the doctrinal wealth of the catechetical exposition. It exhorts, announces, teaches, and finally leads to the very heart of the mystery.[5] Thirdly (though

[5] J. Gelineau, "L'homélie forme plénière de la prédication", *La Maison-Dieu*, 82 (1965), pp. 29-42.

not in order of importance), is the special function of the homily
in integrating the different contributions which each member of
the liturgical assembly can and must offer to the others in terms
of interpretation of the word of God, and mutual consolation.
The homily accepts, discerns and gathers all these into a unity
greater than any discrepancies that may exist. Through this unity,
all are linked with the faith of the whole Church.

To carry out its task, the homily must not be based on an interpretation of the Bible which is purely literal or allegorical or
moral. Rather, it must accept what is good in each one of these
kinds of exegesis and tend towards *anagogia*, i.e., comprehensive-
ness and guidance. Expounding first the meaning of the words of
the celebration, it leads the hearers to a believing assimilation of
their content, a praise-giving celebration of the word as a divine
gift, and the conversion of the life-giving power of the word into
practical reality. In this, it helps to make the word of God,
whether proclaimed, celebrated or lived, what it basically must be
—the means by which we are given the ultimate meaning of
faithful existence.

The homily must be concerned with life, if it is to recover its
liberating power and make a real social and political impact.
Some qualifications to this statement will apply in practice. The
matters that can be touched on in a homily will not refer to problems which affect only one person or a few persons in the community: they must involve everyone, though obviously not to the
same extent for each individual. They must also be situations
which urgently need clarification from the word of God but at
the same time are not going to be reduced to "moral" problems
or cases. They must always relate at a profound level to human
attitudes of mind which have to do with the essential mentality
of the gospel. As to how this gospel light can shine through what
is said, it seems to me that the homily can speak of everything
that can only express one thing: the message of the gospel. The
preacher has no right to put forward his own opinions, or
opinions designed to fit his audience, as the only ones which
harmonize with the law of God. Also, the greatest respect must
always be shown to the word of God; it must always be put in
first place, not the particular subject under consideration. Here
again, however, the temptation must be resisted of using the

Bible to solve all our problems. An effort must always be made to grasp the evangelical attitude revealed in the concrete text, and apply it to the actual situation. What matters most in this task of getting to know the biblical facts is not so much the detail of the circumstance as the profound attitude which God demands, proposes or awakens in men who receive his liberating influence. The only guarantee that we will discover in the actual event of God's call to conversion is our ability to live in tune with these attitudes.[6]

"All these reflections so far presuppose that the preacher and the Church whose voice he sets out to be do not abdicate the task of living immersed in the collective human experience. Otherwise, the existential humus will be lacking, in which the evangelic word can take root. Any corrective which is at odds with experience can justifiably be challenged for that very reason. On the other hand if one shares in common existence one can appreciate the contrast between theory and practical living. The way is then open, not only to say what must be, but to put forward new moral values. The gospel is not a collection of recipes for the solution of problems, but an ethos that must be confronted with the experience of life; in this way its ethic content is shaped and moulded in the course of history. The task of criticism, stimulus, vigilance and restless scrutiny presupposes and requires continual self-criticism on the part of the Church and of those whose duty it is to proclaim the message. Any challenge or interpellation from the standpoint of faith loses its force if solidarity is preached but not practised, liberty is preached when oppression is inflicted, the social and political dimension is preached but the faith is lived at a private, individual level. Every call to conversion must go out to oneself as well. In this kind of dialectic, the preaching of the Church can proclaim the word in all its breadth and implications, with sincerity and efficacy."[7]

Translated by J. P. Donnelly

[6] L. Llopis, "Exégesis bíblica y homilía litúrgica", *Phase*, 11 (1971), pp. 527–41.
[7] J. A. Gimbernat, "Predicación y crítica social", *Phase*, 10 (1970), p. 392.

Jürgen Moltmann

The Liberating Feast[1]

IN Europe, feasts were driven out of public life by the Reformation, puritanism and industrialization. The modern world of work required life to be rationalized in terms of its goal, means and success.[2] For men who adapted and accepted the discipline, the games in feasts seemed childish.[3] The more they came to see the meaning of their lives in calculated ends, the less meaning they saw in the purposelessness and uselessness of feasts. For these modern men the Protestantism of the Enlightenment reduced the liturgies of Christian worship to doctrinal and moral instruction, and excluded hymns and doxologies as superfluous.[4] In this respect, feasts, games and the liturgies of Christian worship are today in the same position. However meaningful they may be in themselves, outwardly they seem purposeless.

Today, however, with growing criticism of this world of goals, performance and success which increasingly seems to impoverish human life, the question of a rebirth of feasts in culture, of a capacity for play in life and of a capacity for liturgy in the representation of Christian freedom is acquiring a new importance.[5]

---

[1] The ideas discussed in this article are set out in more detail in J. Moltmann, *Die ersten Freigelassenen der Schöpfung* (Munich, ³1972).
[2] See Max Weber, *The Protestant Ethic and the Spirit of Capitalism.*
[3] J. Huizinga, *Homo Ludens. Vom Ursprung der Kultur* (1956).
[4] P. Graff, *Die Geschichte der Auflösung der alten gottesdienstlichen Formen in der ev. Kirche Deutschlands* I (1921), II (1939).
[5] On this see Harvey Cox, *The Feast of Fools. A Theological Essay on Festivity and Fantasy* (Cambridge, 1969); D. L. Miller, *Gods and Games: Towards a Theology of Play* (New York, 1970); R. E. Neale, *In Praise of*

Industrial society directed men's interests exclusively to the conquest and control of the world. As long as there existed a shortage of necessities which could be overcome by work, economy and industry were all-important. But once it becomes possible to satisfy elementary needs there is room for a shift of interest from the production of life to its representation, and so to a rebirth of festivity in culture and religion.[6] The path of the total liberation of man from want, oppression and abstinence is different from that of life enacting itself in freedom, but this path cannot reach its goal without being itself a foretaste and anticipation of that freedom.[7] Only the means justify the end—not the other way round—and the goal is only made credible by the path to it. This is why struggles for freedom must constantly be accompanied by the feast of freedom so that the feasts do not become remote from the world and the struggles obsessed with it.

To discover the liberating feast we need: (1) a functional and critical analysis of the present-day social significance of the feast, (2) a theological description of the event of divine liberation which is to be celebrated in and as the feast and (3) an assessment in terms of practical theology of its liberating effect.

I. FUNCTIONAL ANALYSIS

From the earliest times religious celebrations have belonged to the category of ritual.[8] Functional analysis shows that rituals provide historical continuity amid changing periods and generations. Rituals also integrate individuals into groups and groups into larger associations. They also give an order to historical time and the social environment. They heal breaches and settle conflicts. Even today rituals give life order, and in crises give it

---

Play. *Toward a Psychology of Religion* (New York, 1969); G. M. Martin, *Wir wollen hier auf Erden schon* . . . (Stuttgart, 1970).

[6] This distinction between production and representation (reproduction) has been developed with particular subtlety by H. Plessner, *Zwischen Philosophie und Gesellschaft* (Bern, 1953).

[7] The connection between liberating feast and liberation struggle is demonstrated by J. H. Cone, *The Spirituals and the Blues. An Interpretation* (New York, 1972).

[8] For a functional investigation of ritual see Emile Durkheim, *Grundformen des religiösen lebens* (1970).

meaning. In addition to these practical functions, religious rituals and forms of worship also have the gratuitous function of representing existence and its experiences. For this reason, functional analysis cannot fully explain its "demonstrative, existential value" (J. Buytendijk).

In pre-Christian and non-Christian cultures, worship is the feast of the gods.[9] In this feast, the pure origin of the world returns and renews life. As a symbol of the world centre, the cultic place turns chaos into an ordered cosmos. The cultic times turn the flowing time of impermanence into the cycle of the "eternal return of the same". Gods and men come together in sacred places and at sacred times as in the primal event. The myth tells the story of the primal event; the cultic liturgy enacts it. The feast catches men up in the origin, where everything is "as on the first day". In this way the feast is a renewal. It celebrates the *restitutio in integrum*.

The modern world of work deprived the feast of its character as a renewal of the origin. The reproduction of life through work put a stop to the festive renewal of life from a transcendental source. Feasts, arts and holidays were given new functions in the service of the world of work. Formally, they became a suspension of the laws and attitudes which regulate daily life.[10] This suspension is often held to perform a useful political and psychological function by providing outlets.[11] All forms of repressive authority must provide outlets from time to time so that the aggressions they build up can be safely worked off. Oppressed people need "bread and circuses" to enable them to endure their oppression. The same applies in psychology to forced abstinence. Without the opening of outlets from time to time the psychological balance which constitutes self-control cannot be maintained. But where feasts, games and leisure act as outlets they are the instruments of a domination which is incompatible with

[9] See, for example, E. Hornung, *Geschichte als Fest* (Darmstadt, 1966); K. Kerényi, "Vom Wesen des Festes", *Antike Religion* (Munich, 1971), pp. 43–67; M. Eliade, *The Myth of the Eternal Return* (London, 1955).

[10] György Lukacs, *Aesthetik*, Teil 1, 2 (Neuwied, 1963), pp. 577 ff. discusses this "role of the aesthetic sphere as suspension". In the aesthetic act man rests from the pressure of action.

[11] See F. Flögel, *Geschichte des Groteskekomischen. Ein Beitrag zur Geschichte der Menschheit* (Liegnitz and Leipzig, 1788).

freedom. The second function of this suspension may be described as "release". Since everyday life is dominated by tension, responsibility and pressure for achievement, there is a need for periodic release and relaxation. "Holidays" are needed to restore energy. Many people expect Sunday worship to do this for them, and that is one reason why provocative experiments with liturgy are rarely accepted. Both these functions are open to the suspicion that feasts, games and acts of worship do more than compensate for the inadequacies and failures of regulated life by creating an unreal dream-world of freedom: "Freedom exists only in dreams and beauty blooms only in poems" (Schiller).

Today this "opium of the people" is only rarely produced by religions. The manufacturers of dreams and ideologies are much better at it. Contact with freedom in the form of outlets, relaxation and compensation is certainly an alienated contact with freedom, but even unfree contact with freedom is nevertheless contact with freedom and this should not be forgotten.

The alienation of the sort of contact with freedom I have described can be broken with feasts games and acts of worship reveal alternatives to the everyday world of work and make them accessible. They then come to have a similar function to the technique which sets up an unusual "counter-culture" (McLuhan) in opposition to the usual human environment in order to stimulate creative freedom by deliberate confrontation. They are no longer just instruments of the reproductive imagination, working off the boredom of everyday life, but of the productive imagination which investigates and explores the limits of future freedom. They are now no longer dealing with the unreal possibilities of the present, but with the real possibilities of the future. They do not make up for present unfreedom with a dream of freedom, but lift the ban of the unalterability of life by encouraging people to think of real liberation. Release, outlets and compensation have a stabilizing effect on the world of work and domination. By providing anticipation and room for alternatives and experiment, feasts and acts of worship bring a hitherto unknown freedom into unfree life. When feasts and worship make it possible to experience quite new possibilities and powers of liberation, the ban of fate and the feeling of individual impotence are lifted.

A functional theory normally starts from the present world of work and sees only the service function feast, and worship perform for that world. In so doing it supports the forces working for the stabilization of that world. In contrast, a critical theory must start from the freedom experienced in feasts and worship and investigate its liberating action on men and situations. The two approaches complement each other in that critical reflection has become essential to reveal the mostly unconscious context of feasts and worship in modern life if the feast of freedom is to have a liberating and not a stabilizing effect. But both theories must go further and provide a material description of the actual experience of freedom in question. Only on the basis of such a description can the functions appropriate to this freedom be found and defined. What is the freedom which is celebrated in Christian worship and which gives us the right to call that worship a "liberating feast"?

II. THEOLOGY OF LIBERATION

Christian worship is and always has been in essence the feast of Christ's resurrection from the dead.[12] For this reason it was celebrated on the first day of the week, Sunday, at sunrise. It was a eucharistic celebration with bread and wine. Worship and eucharist combine in a special way past and eschatological future, recollection and hope.[13] In the language of Ernst Bloch, the representation of the suffering and death of Jesus is hope in the mode of recollection, and the representation of the future of the Lord is recollection in the mode of hope. He who was crucified by this world is expected to come as the liberator of this world, and the liberation he brings about is already experienced in the powers of the Spirit. In the combination of past and future, recollection and hope, the present is lived as the enjoyment of this

---

[12] For more details of this understanding of the resurrection of Christ, see J. Moltmann, *Der gekreuzigte Gott* (Munich, 1972).

[13] Thomas Aquinas, *Summa Theol.* III, q. 60, ad 3: "Sacramentum est et signum rememorativum ejus quod praecessit, scilicet passionis Christi, et demonstrativum ejus quod nobis efficitur per Christi passionem, scilicet gratiae, et prognosticum, id est praenuntiantem futurae gloriae"; "A sacrament is a sign which recalls a past event, the passion of Christ, indicates the effect of Christ's passion in us, i.e., grace, and foretells, that is, heralds, the glory that is to come."

freedom. The raising of the crucified into the coming glory of God is recalled as the source of this freedom, and its effects are experienced in faith. The coming of Christ is looked for to bring the perfection of freedom to the whole of enslaved creation (Rom. 8. 19). In worship and in the eucharist men are taken up into this eschatological process of the setting free of the world to be the kingdom of glory. They celebrate this freedom in eschatological rejoicing and bring it into the world by taking up their crosses. The recollection of the suffering of the crucified rules out a view of the feast as an escape from the painful conditions of earthly life. It is more like the silent suffering of mankind and creation made audible in the groaning of the Spirit. Hope in the risen Christ rules out mere lamentation over this suffering without hope or denouncing its causes without joy. Faith in the raising of Christ from the dead leads to a firm solidarity with the un-redeemed world. With freedom so near, the chains begin to rub. But at the same time it releases us from the law and fate of this world into a new creative life. Joy at the presence of freedom through reconciliation is thus mixed with pain at the presence of unfreedom and hope of the world's release from it.

In the perspective of ordinary history, the resurrection of Christ cannot be proved and makes no sense. To prove some-things always means to add something new to the system of what is already known. But if the resurrection of Christ presents a challenge to the familiar system of the ordinary world, with its cycle of law, guilt and death, it cannot be proved in terms of that system. But the position becomes quite different when we look at ordinary history in terms of the resurrection of Christ.[14] Then what is ordinary makes no sense. The old law is annulled. The inescapability of history is destroyed. From this point of view faith means recognizing the creative freedom of the God who makes the impossible possible, calls into existence what does not exist (Rom. 4. 17) and exalts what is despised in the world (1 Cor. 1. 26–31), and sharing in this creative power of his. Freedom is now no longer "the understanding of necessity", but creative power for a new life. It follows from this that the raising of the crucified

[14] See the discussion of the "theology of hope", in R. Garaudy, *L'Alternative* (Paris, 1972).

reveals the eschatological alternative to the system of this world and society. As this alternative it is celebrated with feasting and introduced into unfree life as an anticipation of freedom. It is impossible to talk about the resurrection of Christ unless one has experienced the Spirit of the resurrection in faith and obtained the freedom of this Spirit. The process of the new creation of the world begins with the resurrection of Christ through this experience of freedom in faith. It will be completed when the dead too receive justice, and "every rule and every authority and power", and death itself, is destroyed, "that God may be everything to everyone" (1 Cor. 15. 28).

The experience of freedom acquired through faith in the resurrection of Christ mocks "the world with its great wrath" (P. Gerhard). From the earliest times, Easter hymns have celebrated the victory of life in an exorcism of mockery, ridiculing death, pouring scorn on hell and facing the lords of this world without fear.[15] This can be seen as early as the first surviving Easter hymn in 1 Cor. 15. 55–57: "Death is swallowed up in victory. O death, where is thy victory? O death, where is thy sting?... But thanks be to God, who gives us the victory through our Lord Jesus Christ." Easter sermons in the Middle Ages and even later are said to have begun with a joke. Laughter takes away the seriousness of a threat, disarms it. It shows unassailable freedom where the enemy had expected fear and guilt. And when the foundation of all threats against man is death, Easter is really the beginning of the liberation of the oppressed. The liberating feast of the resurrection of Christ stands between the slavery of the past and the coming life in freedom. It manifests the joy of freedom, since there is no other way in which the experience of freedom can be comprehended.

Falling at the beginning of the week, the liberating feast points symbolically back to the creation at the beginning (2 Cor. 4. 6), and for this reason faith regards the creation of all things as a liberation. Called by the creator's word out of non-existence into existence and out of chaos into order, all things are created in freedom and destined for freedom. Seen as the creation of God's freedom, the existence of the world is not necessary. No purpose

---

[15] Flögel, *op. cit.*, gives many examples of the *risus paschalis*.

is served by the existence of something where once there was nothing. Theology has described this freedom of the world by saying that if creation had been necessary to God he would not have been the creator. If it had been simply an accident, the creator would not have been God but an unpredictable demon. Nor is creation a necessary surrender of anything by God, or an outflow from the fullness of his essence. God is free, but he does not act arbitrarily. When he creates something that is not divine but also not nothingness, that thing has its origin not in itself but in God's pleasure. God freely creates a creation which corresponds to him. Between arbitrariness and necessity, theology has taught us to see the world as a creative game of his pleasure, which is undetermined but nevertheless in the deepest possible way corresponds to him. Hugo Rahner has remarked that when we say that the creating God is at play, what is concealed in this image is the metaphysical insight that the creation of the world and man was an action which made sense for God but was in no way necessary for him.[16]

The liberating feast of the resurrection of Christ points back to the creative mystery of God and stresses that creation had the unforced gratuitousness of a game. Pleasure in the experience of liberation combines with the pleasure of the whole creation in existence. The demonstrative value of being which exists in all forms of life is given a voice in man's joy in his liberation, or, put the other way round, that experience of freedom discovers its cosmic dimensions. It is for this reason that the Easter liturgy of the Orthodox Church has always consciously taken the form of a cosmic as well as a human liturgy. The status of a child of God which is a symbol of man's liberation has a counterpart in the free creation and "play as a world symbol".[17] The discovery of these cosmic dimensions in the liberating feast implies an alternative for everyday dealings with the world. Where these dealings are dominated in our society by the exploitation of nature as an object, the feast reveals possibilities of harmony and co-operation which recognize nature as a partner.

The celebration of the resurrection of Christ in the liberating

[16] Hugo Rahner, *Man at Play* (London and New York, 1965).
[17] E. Fink, *Spiel als Weltsymbol* (Stuttgart, 1960).

feast as an anticipation of the universal resurrection from the dead points forward to the creation of the last times, to the new creation of all things, the kingdom of God, the kingdom of glory. Christian eschatology has never represented this end of history as the result of historical struggles or the goal of human moral efforts. It has regarded it as the end of the history of domination and work, and described it in aesthetic categories—as a song of endless joy, the dance of the redeemed, with infinitely varied patterns, the perfect harmony of body and soul, nature and man, in the revealed glory of God. It has never painted the joy of redeemed existence in the colours of this life, stained as it is with weariness, toil and guilt, but with what Ernst Bloch called "everyone's childhood vision", unforced laughter, total admiration and new innocence. The visions of redeemed existence are not taken from the world of struggle and work, but from the world of basic childish trust. The game of glory will put a stop to the suffering of struggle and the boast of victories. The risen one whose feast is celebrated is "the leader of the mystical dance" (Hippolytus) and his Church is his "bride and partner".[18] What is called "the end of history" is, for a Christian understanding, not an end in the sense of a goal, but release from a life subordinated by the law to goals and achievements into the joy of God. In this joy, according to Luther, man will "play with heaven and earth and the sun and all creatures. All creatures will live, love and rejoice, and will laugh with you and you with them, even in the body."[19] The liberating feast is a foretaste, a glimmering, but also a real beginning, of this new world of joy in total freedom. The liberating feast is the anticipation of the festive, free world of God. This discovery in it of the eschatological dimensions of freedom reveals another alternative to daily life and this life is seen not so much a long march as a prelude, not as a preparation but a foreshadowing of the coming life of joy. What is left in eternity out of the flow of time depends on grace, the luck of love and the experiences of liberation, but not on proud achievement or effort. That freedom already shows itself here and now in the flesh, in the natural grace, spirit and love-

[18] Quoted in Rahner, *op. cit.*
[19] Martin Luther, *Weimarer Ausgabe* 39, I, 48.

liness of the life Dostoievski depicted in the prostitute Sonia. "Beauty will redeem the world."[20] In the experience of the faith of the resurrection God himself, as the essence of freedom, appears "beautiful" because he radiates joy (Karl Barth). Since the "kingdom of God" has been so moralized that it no longer seems to require freedom, but only obedience, it is time to rediscover the glory of God which makes us free to be happy.[21] Without this discovery there can be no liberating feast.

III. Practical Effects of Liberation

If we now try to investigate the action of the feast of the resurrection of Christ, the first thing we find is the influence of aesthetic categories on moral ones. The moral seriousness of liberation and improving the world has a tendency to totalitarianism. It leaves no time for festive joy and spoils the sense of beauty. When Christian faith bows to the moral law it feels compelled to balance the law of the old world against the law of the new. The result of this, however, is not freedom but a new unfreedom. The Christian Church then becomes obsessed with the need to make itself useful all over the place in order to justify its existence, and so loses the alternative it has to offer. If, instead, it could see the liberating feast as the expression of its experience of freedom, it could break through the moral and political seriousness of history-making by a relaxed joy in existence itself. This would not in any way make such determination to struggle superfluous. Far from that, it would preserve it and protect it from its totalitarian frenzy on the one hand and its temptation to despair on the other. By being freed from its obsession with achievement, the revolutionary spirit would be preserved from giving up before the unachievable. Aesthetic pleasure in freedom has a liberating effect on the liberation struggles which have to be fought. It removes the alienations which are always created in such struggles. It works like the gospel on the law or the in-

[20] J. Moltmann, "Dostoiewski und die 'Theologie der Hoffnung", in *Entscheidung und Solidarität Festschrift für Joh. Harder* (Wuppertal, 1973), pp. 163–78.
[21] An inspiration in this task is provided by Hans Urs von Balthasar's great work, *Herrlichkeit, eine theologische Ästhetik* I (1961).

dicative of new existence on the imperative of the renewal of life.

In the light of the resurrection hope, freedom has two sides. It lives in liberating protest and it lives on the superabundance of the future.[22] Because resurrection overcomes death, its protest resists death and the power of death in the midst of life. It resists the private death of apathy, the social death of the abandoned and the noisy death of bombs. It protests against all power which is based on the threat of death. Freedom lives in resistance to inward and outward denial of freedom. But freedom does not live on this protest, but on the hope of a greater fulfilment. "Much more", says Paul again and again when talking about the difference between "freedom from" and "freedom for" (Rom. 5. 15–20). God's grace is greater than men's sins. His freedom is more than freedom from oppression. His new creation is greater than man's past. This has been called the "economy of unearned fulfilment" (P. Ricoeur). The "but" with which we resist oppression is only the dark side of the hope in the "much more". Resistance must be rooted in hope if it is not to decay into hate and revenge. Hope must lead to this resistance if it wants to avoid turning into the opium of the people. The superabundance of hope can be celebrated only in festive ecstasies. These produce constantly new forms of opposition to all the forms of unfree life. Even if the liberating feast cannot be given a complete historical equivalent in liberation movements, it is still not meaningless because it enables us to see better opportunities in the future. Seen as a liberating feast, Christian worship becomes a "messianic intermezzo".[23]

Translated by Francis McDonagh

[22] P. Ricoeur, "La liberté selon l'espérance", in *Le Conflit des interprétations* (Paris, 1969), pp. 393–415.
[23] A. A. van Ruler, *Droom en Gestalte* (Amsterdam, 1947); *Gestaltwerdung Christi in der Welt* (Neukirchen, 1956).

David Power

The Song of the Lord
in an Alien Land

I WOULD LIKE to introduce this reflection on liturgy and politics with three quotations, which in their own way focus the problem.

"The language of many hymns, liturgies and homilies sound to secular man, engaged in the task of creating a new world, as the voice of a strange and remote world."[1]

"The liturgy of men whose politics is one of genocide and brutality can only be a liturgy of the mask."[2]

"It is our concern that across confrontations and even oppositions, the ecclesial community can witness in the very depths of the divergences between its members to its tension towards unity, a unity already mysteriously given whenever the eucharist is celebrated and which awaits its manifestation when the Lord returns."[3]

These three quotations put a number of questions to us. In the first place, when Christians worship can they do so as a people who bring their concerns of daily life with them, conscious of the part they have in shaping the world and its history? Does the language of liturgical expression relate to the world in which they live and work, does it open up dimensions of political involvement in so doing? Are they prompted by liturgy to a re-appraisal of their stance on political questions, or do they use it

---

[1] R. Alves, *Teologia della Speranza Umana* (Brescia, 1971) (translated from the English, *A Theology of Human Hope*), p. 56.
[2] G. Gillan, "Symbol: Word for the Other", *Worship*, 41 (1967), p. 281.
[3] Episcopat Français, "Pour une Pratique chrétienne de la Politique", *Documentation Catholique*, 69 (1972), p. 1011.

as a mask over what are their real interests and desires? In political and social matters, is it possible to harmonize pluralism and unity, and that at the very heart of religious expression, which is the eucharist?

I. Dominant Direction and Specific Project

A recent article in another issue of *Concilium*[4] mentions that in certain forms of modern music expression is given to general dissatisfaction with the world and society in which we live. One of these is hard rock, which is used as a form of protest against the meaninglessness of much that is embodied in cultural and social institutions. Sometimes it does not go beyond protest, but it can at times express another set of values, another dream to replace the technological. Some of the Beatles' songs have been quoted as an example of such alternative vision.[5] They are songs which celebrate the virtues of domesticity and individual freedom, in a way which suggests not only a liberation from technology but also a withdrawal from social concern. A lack of public conscience seems to accompany the lack of enthusiasm for the possibilities of science and organization. Needless to say, were such an attitude to be widely adopted, there would be inevitable practical and long-range consequences for society.

A national anthem is one of the modes in which a nation's aspirations are couched. It embodies a people's self-image and expresses a view of things within which particular concerns are approached. One cannot be unaware of the values it enhances and the pervading influence of the self-image on sundry matters. In Ireland at the present juncture of its history, to take but one example, the worry of some is that were its *Soldiers' Song* to capture the minds of the people it could only bolster deeds of violence and retribution.

These two instances have been quoted to illustrate how individual actions and projects may be influenced by a long-range view of things. In a vague and general way, people pursue ideals

[4] J. Gill, "Religious Expression and the Language of Popular Culture", *Concilium*, May 1973 (American edn., Vol. 85).

[5] G. O'Collins, *Man and His New Hopes* (New York, 1969), p. 9.

and purposes in all that they do. They know that particular choices necessarily bear reference to the long-term view. They accept to be challenged in what they do in terms of a vision and a horizon. At the same time, the horizon or general direction is not easy to get into clear focus. It does not sustain detailed or restrictive description. It is much better expressed in poetic images, in myths and legends, in song and festival. Yet it is unquestionable that the expression of this vision as a general direction in which people are heading is an important factor in inspiring and motivating daily actions and short-range schemes.

We are here dealing with a distinction which may be called a distinction between dominant direction and specific project.[6] It is one which can be used in a basic statement on the relation between politics and liturgy. In liturgy, the church community expresses the direction of the life which it pursues in faith and hope. Within the orbit of such a vision and range of values, it faces the question of political involvement.

As soon as this has been said, the word *politics* hangs ambiguously in the air. Evidently it refers to the concrete. It is the art of the possible, a matter of responsible action and specific planning for decipherable ends. How much, however, does it cover of man's activity and how dependent is it on a vision of the ultimate?

The relation between liturgy and politics can be discussed only within the broader context of the relation between gospel and politics. As the meaning of the word has been discussed in an earlier article,[7] let me just make a few observations relevant to my own reflection on the matter.

Sometimes in the argument about gospel and politics, the word *politics* is "defused" by a considerable broadening of its scope. It is made to cover the whole social dimension of human endeavour. It vaguely includes all the issues discussed, for example, in the second part of *Gaudium et Spes*. Hence it becomes almost synonymous with the common good, which "embraces the sum of those conditions of social life by which individuals,

[6] Cf. R. Hart, *Unfinished Man and the Imagination* (New York, 1968), pp. 219-27.

[7] H. Schmidt, *Politieke gedragslijnen van de hedendaagse liturgie.*

families and groups achieve their own fulfilment in a relatively thorough and ready way".[8] On the other hand, for a number of Christian communities worried about gospel and politics, or about the expression of their political interest in liturgy, the meaning of the word is much more specific. It has to do with government and the nature of the regime under which a country lives. It includes the way the people take part in this. It refers to the ways in which a political system affects home issues and international relations. The interest of these Christians is the part which their faith prompts them to take in strictly political questions, their stance on matters decided by legislation, rule and government administration. How, for example, does a Christian community face the problem of an unjust and oppressive regime? How does it think about the Vietnam war or the communist regime in Poland? What must it do about international affairs and the agreements between governments which affect the distribution of economic wealth and the balance of power?

It seems to me, then, that there are two separate problems, the second a specification of the first. The gospel gives the twin precepts of love of God and love of neighbour. This obviously means that a Christian always takes the intersubjective into account, and we can add moreover, without risk of too much debate, a necessary predilection for the unfavoured and the poor. Hence the two questions: What does this imply in terms of a need to take a part in social issues, understanding these in the broad sense of *Gaudium et Spes*? And what does it imply by way of a spur or a compulsion to take a more direct part in politics?

To put it another way, we can ask whether the gospel obliges us to take an active interest and part in such matters. Or is it simply that when the interest is there, it receives inspiration and direction from the gospel? And dependent on the answer to these questions, does the dominant direction of Christian living expressed in liturgy have any bearing on such matters?

Personally, I do not think that the answers to this problem are fully clear. What I am doing is to propose certain lines of reflection, which may be helpful.

[8] Second Vatican Council, *Gaudium et Spes*, 74.

II. LITURGY, HOPE AND FREEDOM

As has often been repeated, and that within the context of politics, liturgy is a celebration of Christian hope. To use the terminology already adopted, it gives the dominant eschatological direction within which specific operations are planned.

As Paul Ricoeur indicates, a primary reflection on symbols, particularly on those of evil, allows for a self-appropriation of one's actions in an ethical and moral sense.[9] It alerts men to their responsibility in causing evil and calls upon them to do something to eliminate it. In a sense of shared guilt and responsibility, a community can take stock of what may be done in a concrete way. It requires a second and more pondered reflection to take account of the elements in the symbols and myths of evil which have been left out of consideration in the search for responsible action. Place must be left for the ambiguous and unknown, the uncontrollable and unverifiable; the control of evil lies beyond the powers of man, just as its exact origins are indecipherable and its precise nature cannot be mapped only in terms of the suffering it imposes. Likewise, in the achievement of responsible and ethical action there is something in man which remains unsatisfied and a dimension of his sin which is not acquitted. This is the element of desire which is somehow present in every deliberation and choice and the sense of having offended a transcendent call. Man is not justified by ethics, or by law and obligation, but by the spirit which pursues the object of desire, drawn by love. To keep this alive, because of its very ambiguity and fragility, symbols are necessary, symbols which allow for the constant appropriation of one's acts as acts of desire. Through this appropriation of desire, man becomes aware that he pursues an object beyond visible limits. In hope, he answers to the call of another, the Other who addresses himself to man as Father in the Christian kerygma.

This is where we come to grips with what is the most specific and distinctive feature of the Christian gospel. God himself dwells in the heart of man, giving form to his desires, and moving him towards the only object worthy of his heart, which is God him-

[9] P. Ricoeur, "Herméneutique des symboles et réflexion philosophique", in *Le conflit des interprétations* (Paris, 1969), pp. 283–329.

self. It is the interiorization and appropriation of one's own desires, the realization of the self as created in the image of the Son through the indwelling of the Spirit, which is the ultimate freedom of the Christian man. This is the most religious aspect of the Christian gospel, and it is at the same time paradoxically the most important politically. The freedom which is worth seeking is not in the long run freedom from political oppression, freedom from economic slavery, freedom from the constraints of poverty, freedom of speech or freedom of gathering. It is the inner freedom which allows a man to be master of his own destiny, and this he can be only by that self-appropriation which allows him to know himself as transcendent. All the other freedoms are relevant and important in as much as they create the environment in which this is possible. Their suppression is an injustice because it hinders a people from being its own master. To stifle people's minds, to subject them to a machine-like efficiency, to deprive them of the means or the ease to take thought, is the greatest crime. It is only on condition that they are able to interiorize God as the force and object of their own desire and autonomous responsibility that people can really shape their own history.

Such a realization in many a given situation will certainly raise specific political questions, and will prompt to action on particular issues. On the other hand, it cannot claim the complete gospel sanction for any particular action since the eschatological perspective also gives a sense of the relative. The realization that the Father is the only object of man's transcendental desire serves to relativize all particular political strategies. There is only one Absolute, and all created things are relative and passing, of worth in as much as they enable man to realize himself in the quest of the ultimate. It is the paradox of Christian truth that what is important in this world is also trivial. This is the sense of so many of the apparent contradictions of scriptural images. Man cannot add one hair to his head by taking thought, yet not one falls without God knowing. He must calculate well before he builds a tower, yet he will never succeed in building it unless he renounces all he possesses. The community that comes together to pray upon the Bible is faced with juxtapositions which seem absurd, with the images of irony which serve to keep all things in due proportion.

As it is hinted in the gospels, the eucharist itself is a kind of parody for there the master serves at table instead of being served, the poor man is adorned with the rich garment and put in the first seat, while the rich man dons sackcloth and sits at the foot of the table.

III. LITURGY AND THE CONCRETE: THE INTERLACING OF HORIZON AND SPECIFIC PROJECT

As Edward Schillebeeckx remarks, "language, including the language of faith, becomes meaningless, in the sense in which linguistic analysts use the term, if it does not contain a recognizable reference to man's experience in the world".[10] This holds good for liturgy, as for all forms of kerygma, catechesis, prayer and profession of faith. But it would be a mistake to think that if the right ideology is expressed in liturgy it will automatically effect change. The anthropologist Victor Turner has criticized current liturgical reform in the Catholic Church on the grounds that it is inspired by a mixture of structural functionalism and behaviourism.[11] It is based, he says, on the assumption that through ritual man can be conditioned to the social change taking place and that this can be promoted through ritual. In other words, if the right things are said the right things will happen. In effect, this is nothing but a refined continuation of the naïveté often associated with the *ex opere operato* approach to sacraments. The principal difference is the enlargement of the concept of grace and the search for a more intelligible expression of what is taken to be happening.

A more circumspect approach needs to be taken to liturgy's reference to the concrete. It is one which takes account of the way that dominant direction and specific project interlace. People do not first spell out their horizons and values, and then plan particular acts accordingly. In fact, specific commitments and choices precede the explication of general horizon, which is worked out largely by way of challenge to what a people or com-

---

[10] E. Schillebeeckx, "The Crisis in the Language of Faith as a Hermenutical Problem", *Concilium*, May 1973 (American edn., Vol. 85).

[11] V. Turner, "Passages, Margins and Poverty: Religious Symbols of Communitas", *Worship*, 46 (1972), p. 392.

munity is doing. Inasmuch as it is already there in traditions and cultural institutions, the earlier actions are influenced by it, but each person has to explicate it for himself by questioning the values and meanings which are expressed in his concrete activity. The questioning, if pursued, leads in the direction of an ultimate purpose and discovers a unity giving form to life.

The preaching of Jesus as recorded in the Sermon on the Mount gives us some helpful hints. He presents his hearers with the kingdom by way of a challenge to their concrete actions. The man who wants to divorce his wife is told that they might after all be reconciled: there is another and better way of tackling the problem than that of righteous indignation and the demand for just rights. He who wants to take his neighbour to court is asked why he keeps going to the temple. The one who begrudges his companion on the road an extra mile is mildly scoffed at. He who seethes with anger at his enemy is made to see that there is nothing as poisonous as a justified resentment. Above all, the Jew who holds only another Jew as neighbour and worthy of love has his blindfold removed.

One can talk for ever of the love of God in Jesus Christ, but it takes a parable to make me ask whether this love is present in my daily actions and conduct. This is relevant to liturgy's claim to mediate reality. It claims not only to talk about it but to make it. It purports to allow the subject to express his relation to reality in a self-involving language. To be truly self-involving, it must not only express the horizons of faith but must also involve the daily self in their pursuit. A man needs to be swallowed up in the concrete before you can talk to him of the meaning of life, but he cannot carry on in any human sense without wondering about meaning. Those who come to worship have their interests, their commitments, their values and pursuits. Putting the question of dominant direction to them is a matter of asking what they are aiming at when they do this, that or the other. It should inspire wonder and inquiry, as well as encourage hope. As Bernard Lonergan says,[12] all our questions are questions about God but they start off by being questions about everyday life and its eventualities. In a very particular way, Christian faith interests us

[12] B. Lonergan, *Method in Theology* (London, 1972), pp. 101–103.

in questions about our neighbour. It is to the transformation of his daily relations and actions that man must first be tempted, in such a way as to open out the possibilities of new horizons and a conversion to new values.

IV. The Memory of Suffering

The very essence of Christian liturgy is the *memoria passionis Domini*. The link between this memory and political life has been so well treated by J. B. Metz,[13] that I find it futile to say very much here. One or two observations will suffice.

The article in this issue of *Concilium* on the symbols of evil reminds us how much the problem of sin and suffering is at the heart of human existence. The Judeo-Christian tradition allows us to glimpse how suffering engenders vital forces of good. It asks strong questions about the sense we make of suffering, both our own and that of other persons. It suggests how values come into being and attitudes are formed in times of stress. Israel's knowledge and love of God often moved forward in the years of her misfortune. It was easy to sing of the Lord as her rock and her strength in days of glory, but what of her song in less happy circumstances? One of the recurrent themes of the Bible is the quest for the meaning of suffering. It is a quest followed in anguish and doubt but which none the less gives rise to the conviction that if lived aright it can lead somewhere meaningful. Its successful outcome is very much linked with the problem of man's inner freedom.

Secondly, it is in Christ's suffering that we see how it is turned into a force for good. The cause and the virtue of Christ's suffering was compassion with suffering mankind: accepting the onslaught of the evil which befell him as the consequence of the evil that was in man, he broke the vicious circle by transforming the evil of his suffering into an act of love. Hence we see the weight of Metz's statement: "The memory of suffering brings a new moral imagination into political life, a new vision of others' suf-

[13] Cf. J. B. Metz, "The Future in the Memory of Suffering", *Concilium*, June 1972 (American edn., Vol. 76).

fering which should mature into a generous, uncalculating partisanship on behalf of the weak and unrepresented".[14]

V. LITURGY, REMEMBRANCE AND HISTORY

We have established the dominant direction given by liturgy through eschatological hope. We have seen that this takes effect in man's life by virtue of concrete and questioning language. We have introduced the actuality of suffering as a necessary part of the pursuit of the general direction. It is now opportune to recall that the cue to a liturgical realism which intrudes upon the political and social scene is the historical dimension of God's revelation. It is also its dilemma, because of an ambiguity we find in Christian tradition when it comes to the affirmation that God is the Lord of history.

For some, the role of the political order is mainly that of containing the corruption of the world, of keeping evil in check. That done, man is free to hear God's word or contemplate the heavenly city, as the case may be. The citizen's duty to the social order is to conform to it—unless it happens to deny the rights of religion and religious practice. He can moreover in unjust situations rely on God as the Lord of history to intervene according to his designs. Ultimately it is He who controls history and the political order, by his unanticipated and gratuitous interventions. The citizen is not excused from healing injustices when he can, but he places his ultimate reliance on God's gratuitous action. This is a long tradition, dating from Augustine and claiming its roots in St Paul, and which finds modern expression in somebody like Jacques Ellul.[15]

In such perspective, to speak of God's revelation in history is only to say that you can date and map the event of the Incarnation and all other revelatory events. Revelation is the word which frees us from space and time by allowing us to transcend them. God's word is in a sense tangential to space and time, it interrupts the flow of history and promises salvation to the man immersed in the cares and anxieties of the world. It is the assurance

[14] *Loc. cit.*
[15] As an example of his writing, cf. J. Ellul, *Politique de dieu politiques de l'homme* (Paris, 1966).

that God is with us, that his word is a word of salvation and that evil shall not triumph.

Others, however, would prefer to see God's revelation as something which comes to us much more definitely *through* history. This perspective seeks to interlock secular activity of every kind, religious or spiritual experience and revelation. In face of evil and suffering, it not only asks trust in God and his saving power. It puts out a plea to take issue with evil, to resist to the point of shedding blood, to upheave the social order in the interests of justice. It claims that these actions are not only an answer to a word of God but that in the actions themselves God speaks to us. Because they involve a movement towards self-transcendence, a spiritual experience takes shape in these actions of history. It is an experience which enables us to know God in the very act of loving our neighbour. This love of neighbour may be of a very domesticated nature, but it may also be practised on the political scene. In either case, it is the reflection on what takes place between men, on the values shown or challenged, on the meaning which is sought, which allows a transcendent movement towards God.

The problem of how God manifests himself in political history stands out most clearly in the case of the Old Testament. On the one hand, God's salvation can be seen as his irruption into history, his intervention to free his people, protect them, punish them, etc. It is the word of promise, command and reprimand which he addresses to them through his prophets. On the other hand, it could be said that the role of the prophet was to make the people reflect upon their experiences of liberation, good fortune, calamity, social change, etc., and to find in these experiences an opening out to the reality of the transcendent God. God is the Lord of history through the engraving of his word on the hearts of men, leading them to gracious self-awareness. The Jewish people learn to see that all historical reality finds meaning only in him, and that it has unity through a meaning which points in the direction of a God who is both immanent and transcendent. The change in their own political fortunes, the attempts at reform of their social order, prompted a self-questioning in terms of values, meaning and direction. The word of God comes through a process of interiorization, so that interiorization is not simply the response to a word but that in which the word is given.

The role of the prophet and the external word, which came from him or from the tradition of a previous generation, called the people to this process of interiorization and so to a new experience of God. It is to reflection on their situation that they were called by the prophet and the religious tradition. This enabled them to see how they stood in relation to God and to grasp the "theological" nature of social order and political event.

There are few direct political implications in the preaching and life of Jesus. The one thing which is clear in his preaching, and then in his death and resurrection, is that the kingdom of God comes by the power of God and in the event of human weakness and self-emptying. He died as a poor man, identified with human poverty. One must then ask what this means for social concern and political action. Once again, do we simply act in response to a word of God or is the response a new experience and discovery of God? We are hard put to know exactly how the word and Spirit of Jesus Christ operate as forces in this world. On the one hand, they may be conceived as irruptions, climactic forces from on high which disturb all human calculations and promise salvation to the believer, a personal or even social victory over the forces of evil which surround him. This would mean awaiting God's intervention in history with a trust which comes from the death and resurrection of Christ. The sense in which man himself is the agent of God's action would be rather limited.[16] On the other hand, serious weight has to be given to the belief in the indwelling Spirit. The power of God changes man himself, not only the events of his history, and the history is changed by the change in man. The experience of God is commensurate with the change in life-style to which the Spirit prompts us. The practice of love of neighbour and concern for justice is not only obedience to a command or a preparation of the ground for God's intervention. It is itself the intervention and the shaping force of history. To say this, is not to reflect a naïve belief that every advancement is the work of God, but means that we are ready to

[16] Alves criticizes J. Moltmann on the basis that his theology ultimately leaves room only for pacificism, because of his stress on the fact that man receives his future from the word of God. According to Alves, this does not permit us to see how God acts through man's own history. Cf. Alves, *op. cit.*, pp. 94–112.

reflect on every fortune or misfortune in reference to the gospel, to question our values and meanings over against the values and meaning incarnate in Jesus Christ and the Christian community. The meaning of history is then sought in the dominant direction of man's movement towards the Father as God of his future.

In face of this enigma, liturgy is easily tempted to adopt an ideology, to force the issue and make us choose sides. This would be to miss the point of liturgy. A major contribution of its remembrance is to make the Christian community avoid polarization through the adoption of opposing ideologies. That is why we must take account of the parabolic nature of liturgical commemoration, and likewise keep stock of the fact that the paradigmatic events commemorated are themselves parabolic in form.[17] The Christ-event is remembered in such a way that it is a perpetual question-mark, questioning even the very questions which we ask ourselves. It is in this way that it keeps us alive to the quest for dominiant direction. Moreover, it is not only Christ but the whole Christian tradition which challenges and questions us: Christ and how our forefathers have lived Christ. By virtue of this prophetic role, our worship does not resolve but keeps us alive to the tension between the hope for the manifestation of God's power and the urge to take action in the power of his Spirit.

In brief, the prophetic character of worship reminds us that human history finds its meaning in the eschatological hope of God. This requires a reflection on the Scriptures which is also the expression of a shared concern and a mutual encouragement. In particular, it should press the question of action on behalf of neighbour. The concerns manifested by the community and its individual members, particularly regarding political action, cannot always be given an easy answer, but the Christian fellowship ought to comfort and strengthen its members in the dilemmas which arise from personal conscience.

VI. THE LIBERATING IMAGE

It is the spirit of the gospel which inspires many Christians

[17] See J. B. Metz, "A Short Apology of Narrative", *Concilium*, May 1973 (American edn., Vol. 85).

with the desire to become politically involved. The events commemorated in worship exact love of the poor and hatred of injustice. They also raise the question: for what? Given justice and
political freedom, what then? When are men free? What is the
very core of freedom in the Spirit?

None of this questioning makes the struggle for justice any less
imperative. It does affect the goals pursued and the means em-
ployed. It alerts to the values which have to be respected at all
times—in the course of the revolution, as well as when it has
been accomplished. It reminds us that we can easily have illusions
about what constitutes freedom, happiness or peace. It keeps these
concepts open, because it insists on speaking in image and narrative, in symbol and mythical story-telling.

One of liturgy's first effects in the political order is the influence exercised over ideas which form a part of political planning. This is because of the imaginative and symbolic form of
liturgical expression. Take the example of a Christian who wants
to take part in the construction of an order of justice and peace.
When he celebrates his quest in liturgy, he is invited to see that
this means partaking in the justice and peace of God. If he thinks
along the lines of the images of Bible and worship, his sense of
justice might get some rude shocks, for he will see that God's
justice is also his mercy. It is not the demand for penalty for the
wrong-doer. It is pardon and reconciliation, obtained indeed at a
price, but at the price of love. The Christian kerygma is that the
death of Christ is an act of love, the suffering taken upon himself
by the one for the many, whereby justice is restored to the world.

It is important to advert to this freeing and enlarging power of
biblical and liturgical images and symbols. This is because of the
ultimate disparity between social structure and religious reality,
between social or political authority and divine authority, between the symbols of social constructs and religious symbols. It
is this disparity which allows the religious man to be basically
independent and critical of any social system or earthly authority.[18] It is clear to him that no social order can embody, or even
leave room for, all the possibilities of a community of persons
formed in the image of God. He knows that every human auth-

[18] Cf. J. Remy, "L'image d'un dieu père dans une société sans père",
Lumière et Vie, 104 (1971), pp. 5-26.

ority can err, that there is a justice which transcends every human justice, that only in the Spirit of the Lord can we discern right and wrong. Every attempt in Christian history to identify an earthly authority, secular or ecclesiastical, with the authority of God had bad effects. Of neither king, bishop nor pope can it be said that he is the "image of the Father", unless we are immediately prepared to break the force of that image by a broader imaginative context, which does not allow the image to freeze or usurp divine rights.[19]

The images of eschatological hope conquer the fear of failure and the fear of the future, and thus the very root and source of violence. In other words, the sense which the liturgy can create of the overriding justice which supersedes any human justice, of a freedom which transcends any humanly won freedom, of an order of which man's order is only an approximation (in other words, of the *divina comedia*), is the best guarantee we have that it is possible to dominate the violence which is inherent in man's instinct for what he deems the "good of order". It is not the violence of the revolt which must be eradicated in the first instance, but the violence inherent in almost any legitimized regime. The concern for order and the search for what is needful to the good working of society provokes the instinct to impose on all a certain conformity. The violence of imposition is then partnered by the violence of punishment, meted out to refractors. Such an instinct can be dominated only by a double countering instinct: the first is the spirit of poverty, possible only when an ethics of responsible action is measured against an ethics of desire and hope, and the second is a genuine care for one's neighbour, which is born out of the memory of suffering.

In Christian symbolism, there is a vast place for the symbols of what Victor Turner has termed the "power of the weak".[20] The suffering, the poor, the sick, the feeble, the young, may well incarnate and bring to being values which are more important to society than the achievements of the strong, the rich, or the acknowledged leaders of society or revolution. The effort required

[19] Even with regard to images of ecclesiastical authority, we find the coupling in Vatican II of "father and brother", and the famous dictum of St Augustine: "a Christian with you, a bishop for you".

[20] Turner, *art. cit.*, p. 395.

in politics to secure power and control could very easily blind men to the values of fraternity, kindness, compassion, humility, purity of heart, contemplation, which are far more readily symbolized in symbols of poverty than they are in symbols of strength or lordship. Needless to say, if these values are engraven in men's hearts they have a vast influence on what is sought in the bettering of a social or economic or educational system.

If I may appeal again to Turner's studies, he makes an important distinction between the values of social structure and *communitas*, and their corresponding symbols, in human society.[21] As he remarks, society is in the first place "a structured, differentiated, and often hierarchical system of politico-legal-economic positions with many types of evaluation, separating men in terms of 'more' or 'less' ".[22] Structure and organization are necessary and indispensable, but place must also be given to the values associated with the word *communitas*. Here the emphasis is on equality, comradeship, intersubjectivity, marginality and liminality. It is in the end more important than structure, and there must always be means whereby to protect it against the possible pressures of structure, means which can even be anti-structural. In his works, Turner shows how these two sets of values are symbolized in some African rituals, and he makes some broader applications, including reference to Christian symbols. For our purpose, it is worth noting that Christian liturgy through its symbols keeps alive the values of *communitas* in their Christian dimension and so provides some antidote to the oppressive possibilities of systems. One consequence is that the social prophet or critic ought to find every encouragement in the church assembly, and the socially feeble can be helped to find their own distinctive place in the humanizing of the world. It is not uninteresting in this regard to note the gospel image of messianic table-fellowship as the meal at which Jesus sat down with publicans and prostitutes, or that of the messianic banquet to which the king invites the blind, the lame and the poor.[23] While much of this ritual of

[21] V. Turner, *The Ritual Process: Structure and Anti-structure* (London, 1969).

[22] *Op. cit.*, p. 96.

[23] It is interesting to compare a statement of M. Douglas, *Natural Symbols: Explorations in Cosmology* (New York, 1970), p. 155: "The way to

communitas is traditional, the surprise element in feast also contributes to the non-structured elements of human living and this too ought to have its place in Christian celebration.[24]

VII. THE NEGATIVE ASPECT: WHERE LITURGICAL EXPRESSION DISTORTS

One of our introductory quotations suggested that politically involved persons find much of our current liturgical expression unreal and irrelevant. This occurs when the language of worship avoids every possible concrete reference to political and social institutions or realities, becomes as it were apolitical. It thus avoids the issue, makes believe that religious practice may be situated in the world but with nothing to do with the direction it takes in secular affairs. For those whose faith teaches them otherwise, this is at best irrelevant and at worst the cause of alienation.

When liturgy adverts to political issues, it can happen, and has so happened, as some articles in this issue show, that God's presence is too closely identified with specific powers and evil with specific events, realities or persons. Good is too sharply divided from evil—not just the values but the incarnational realities. This fails to accept the possibilities, the necessity even of political pluralism. It also fails in the critical function of the gospel with regard to all human enterprise. The Christian community ought never be called together to give unqualified support to a given political regime or a particular social project. It may give encouragement to its members in what they are trying to do, but that does not mean a suspension of its critical faculties.

The worst distortion occurs when in face of injustice and op-

---

humanize the system is to reject equality and to cherish the individual case. The institution which runs by strict adherence to general rules gives up its own autonomy. If it tries to adopt equality or seniority or alphabetical order or any other hard and fast principle for promotion and admission, it is bound to override the hard case. Furthermore, it is bound to abandon its traditions and so its identity and its original, special purposes. For these humanizing influences depend upon a continuity with the past, benevolent forms of nepotism, irregular charity, extraordinary promotions, freedom to pioneer in the tradition of the founders, whoever they were."

[24] For an authoritative statement on the social significance and composition of feast, cf. F. Isambert, art. "Fête", *Encyclopaedia Universalis*, 6 (Paris, 1968), pp. 1046-1051.

pression liturgy becomes a mask for the oppressor and a blindfold for the oppressed. It is a recurrence of pharisaism, religion based on observances, coupled with the refusal to hear the call of the word to question values and social practices. For the oppressed, it is a suppression of any hope of liberation, a false promise which merits all the reproaches levelled against religion as the opium of the people. Though common, this kind of abuse is too obvious to warrant very much comment.

More subtly, liturgical commemoration can suppress certain questions completely. One very relevant example of this is the matter of violence. Attitudes towards it can be so negative and so emotional that they exclude all possibility of a total view of the situation in which it arises. This is helped by the way we can explain God's presence in history, veiling over the violence of Old Testament events. The revolutionary events are described as God's action and all is explained as his work. Was there not, however, much spontaneous violence in the happenings which led to Israel's exodus from Egypt? To what extent were the Jews themselves responsible for some of the atrocities listed among the miracles and plagues, e.g. the killing of the first-born? It is one thing to advocate violence, another to try to understand its origin and its outcome. We do not have to approve Israel's violence and cruelty, but we can understand what they were up against and how the winning of their freedom created a new situation in which they could sort out their relationship to Yahweh. In to-day's political situation, conscientization of the oppressed is risky and explosive, but if the situation does explode the explosion too has its positive aspects and puts some very important questions about the temper and customs of society. The effort to stop violence and to preach our concepts of peace may soon mean stopping it "at all costs". While never advocating or wishing it, we might at times *risk* it rather than risk the permanence of a regime of oppression with its own inherent forms of violence. With this one example, I really want to put the question whether liturgical commemoration and prayer may not interpret both past and present in such a way that it closes off certain vital areas of consideration and prophetic comment.

There is, of course, another extreme and that is to emphasize the ritual of protest to the detriment of effective action. This shows up mostly in non-religious demonstration but can invade liturgy as well. It burns up all energies in protest and leaves only a sad or angry feeling of futility. It forgets that the intentionality of dominant direction requires concretization in specific projects. It forgets that it is not enough to have visions, but that one must ask questions about the values adopted in plans and actions. It is like having a liturgy in which we were to sing only the Lucan maledictions and leave out the beatitudes, only the cursing psalms and not the songs in praise of the just man.

Mary Douglas shows that some religious rituals exemplify dissociation from the society in which a person or group lives.[25] Effervescence, trance, bodily dissociation of any sort which implies a certain loss of control of consciousness, express non-identity and an individual or ghetto world. With regard to West Jamaicans in London, whom she takes as an example, she is careful to say that this is "not a compensation but a fair representation" of how they actually relate to their social environment. In our evaluation of such rites, therefore, we must tread warily. There does seem to be a possible exploitation of rites of dissociation in a compensatory way, or at least in a way which canonizes social isolationism. Hence the attraction of drug, the psychedelic, the use of voodoo, and in liturgy the stress on the awesomeness of mystery, transcendent and other-worldly. But social-functionalism is not the answer either! We cannot implant social consciousness in people's minds by giving it its "correct" expression in prayer and ritual. Again what counts is a challenge, an appraisal of one's position, an invitation to be master of one's own destiny, an enlarging of the image of neighbour.

Religious ritual presents its strongest enticement to abandon social responsibility when it seeks refuge in occult and supernatural powers, which control the world by magic and without human struggle. There always is a tendency to express the sacred in this way and there is no need to belabour the fact that Christianity has known its own superstitions. We also know that when Christian ritual refuses to perform this function, then others arise to substitute for it, whether in the extreme form of devil-worship, or in the taboos, charms, etc., of "non-believers".

[25] M. Douglas, op. cit., pp. 82–98.

VIII. The Symbol of the Father[26]

All that has been said is but an explicitation of what is already implied in the description of the liturgy as worship of the Father, in spirit and in truth. According to the New Testament, true cult is life in the Spirit, the living sacrifice of the Church body, which gives witness to the salvation of God and praises him in song and canticle.[27] Ritual in its turn should be both a eucharistic expression and a transformation of man, through which we become "sons in the Son" and so conform to him in his worship of the Father, which is praise, desire and obedience.

Symbols, we say, make present the reality which they contain. This is not chiefly by representation, but by the communication of experience. In other words, they give a share in the meaningful life-experience of the original reality. The symbol on which all others converge in Christian worship is that of Christ, Son of God incarnate, who is the symbol of the Father. Through his symbolic presence in liturgy, he communicates to his followers his own Son-Father relationship. It is the interiorization or appropriation of this relationship which constitutes the essence of Christian life and makes of the Church a living temple to God's glory. It is a desire in the heart of man, answering to the call and recognition of the Father, bringing to fulfilment man's native capacity for transcendence. This desire and thrust provides life with its dominant direction, and it is within this horizon that all policy touching on man's life on earth can be meaningfully worked out. This is the real basis of the Christian's ethical and spiritual existence. It is the spirit which infuses secular action and daily realities, questioning their values, giving them unity, integrating them into God's kingdom as the field in which man lives out his experience of God with his neighbour. Within this horizon, the memory of suffering is the memory of a son who knows God as the common Father and the common future of all

---

[26] For a good representative position on current studies on the symbol of the Father, see the articles and bibliographical survey in *Lumière et Vie*, 104 (1971).

[27] Cf. S. Lyonnet, "La nature du culte dans le Nouveau Testament", in J.-P. Jossua and Y. Congar, *La Liturgie après Vatican II* (Paris, 1967), pp. 357–84.

men, and whose love therefore takes on the shapes shadowed in
the gospel parable of Matt. 25. 31–46.

IX. Liturgy and Political Pluralism

The final conclusion to this essay is an answer to the last of
our opening questions, and may sound prosaic enough. Is liturgy
possible where there is political pluralism in the community?
Can people be united in one worship when divided on political
issues? Clearly, no such manifestation of unity can be tolerated
where there is evident injustice and where liturgy is used as a
mask to cover evil and spiteful divisions. Where, however, there
is a choice of political possibilities, such as is envisaged by the
French bishops in their declaration on Christians and politics,
then unity in worship is not only possible but necessary. It is then
a recognition that the unity of Christians is more than a unity of
trust and desire than it is agreement on specific policies. Liturgy
is then prophetic, a mutual questioning, a mutual listening and
a mutual encouragement. It is prophetic because it calls on all
participants to accept the relative and inadequate nature of their
own work and compels them to realize that they are always
called into question by God's word and the spirit living in the
community of believers.

What are the practical consequences for liturgy? The first is
the need to give due place to a shared reflection on the word of
God. The second is the nature of the prayer of repentance, which
has to be a real readiness to allow ourselves to be called into question. It takes form as an openness to be converted to the desire
for the Father and as a vivid realization that there is no injustice
in which we do not share, and that we can never pray for the
conversion of another unless we pray first for our own. The third
consequence concerns the nature of the prayer of petition. It is
as much a learning of the way to see our needs and projects in the
context of God's kingdom as it is a specific demand for specific
ends. In the fourth place, the prayer of praise includes hope and
desire, since it praises the God who through history draws us
ever onward towards himself.

In the fifth and final place, we are awakened to the fact that
our prayer is prayer to an unknown God, a wondering recogni-

tion that all our images of God are inadequate, and so must be broken and re-made, and broken and re-made again. It is the measure of our experience of God in our life together that allows us to come closer to him in an enlarged desire. To encompass this, we must pass over into the experience of Jesus Christ and of all who went before us, learning in him and with them to say the simple word, *Abba*.[28]

Only if these five conditions are given sense in our liturgies can we talk of the eucharist as the celebration of a community which in its accepted and fruitful pluralism knows the fundamental unity of God's beloved, the vine which he has bruised but from which his right hand will never stray.

[28] Cf. J. S. Dunne, *A Search for God in Time and Memory* (London, 1967).

Joseph Gelineau

Celebrating the Paschal Liberation

MY THESIS is that the celebration of the risen Christ by the assembly of believers is one of the most effective political actions that men can perform in this world—if it is true that this celebration, by contesting any power system which oppresses mankind, proclaims, stirs up and inaugurates a new order in the created world.

My hypothesis is that the liturgy (which, paradoxically, usually operates these days in accordance with a system which intends its own depoliticization inasmuch as it always implies an unknown politicization) can and must discover the authentic political dimension which is essential to it.

The thesis, though acknowledged by some, is treated by many as a paradox or a provocation. Can there be anything more alien to the political order than the liturgy, celebrating as it does the eternal mysteries in a secularized society which has no interest in liturgy as such? This is an opinion common in the Church as well as outside it. Significantly, totalitarian political regimes which react adversely to the Church begin by forbidding Christians any form of self-organized action in society; they then prohibit or supervise religious instruction and preaching; but in general they allow worship as inoffensive. Moreover they sometimes consider the liturgy to be useful because it inculcates respect for the ruling order and submission to the established powers whatever they may be. No less significant is the ordinary behaviour of Christians who are aware of the demands of the gospel in their lives: they begin by committing themselves to social and political action. Some refer to Scripture for enlightenment, courage and hope. But they often remain mere consumers in a cult which they do not experience as an arena of commitment and criticism. Some, however, have seen that things ought not to be like that; and they start to oppose the way in which our liturgies are put over. They even practise new types of small-group celebration based on certain ideas of the political nature of the liturgy.

My intention here is not to demonstrate my thesis, which emerges from all the preceding articles. But once the political dimension of the liturgy has been accepted, we have to discover how the celebration shows forth or conceals its political implications. The task as such seems to me an impossible one. To succeed I should have to invoke the human sciences of semeiology, linguistics, socio-psychology and cultural anthropology, and it would only be possible to do this here in a fragmentary way. An analysis is, moreover, of real value only if it is made of a specific celebration in a specific socio-cultural context, without any possibility of generalizing.

I shall attempt two things in this article. Firstly, I shall put forward some practical positions or attempts at practical solutions in regard to the relations between liturgy and politics— which seem obviously inadequate. Secondly, I shall outline a general operational model of a celebration in which the political drive is apparent. I shall engage in an analytical hypothesis on the nature of practice, but I shall also affirm that an improved and enlightened practice could correct that hypothesis, or replace it with other, better hypotheses.[1]

I. INADEQUATE SOLUTIONS

1. It is pointless to remain at the stage reached by those who state that liturgy has no political dimension, unless to remark that they are living in a state of unconsciousness or illusion. If the link between the celebration and political realities is not apparent, that is presumably because worship is so integrated into the existing socio-religious ideological system that it bears

---

[1] This subject has been generously discussed together with details of others by B. de Clercq in his article "Political Commitment and Liturgical Celebration", in *Concilium*, April 1973 (American edn., Vol. 84).

witness to it implicitly. Then the cult is an agent of the ruling power, whether ecclesiastical or civil.

Perhaps some readers will cite those Orthodox communities under an oppressive political regime which no longer have any ecclesial sign other than the liturgy. Their traditional and conservative liturgy, bearing firm witness to the mysteries of the faith, but as if withdrawn from time and on the periphery of the enclosing society, will probably be adduced as a proof that Christian worship can continue without any political implication. But assemblies of that kind at least signify that isolated groups are resisting official doctrine. They constitute a major political fact (of which the powers in control are well aware).

2. One very widespread position is that the liturgy as a celebration is not political in itself, and cannot be so, since its concern is that universal and eternal salvation offered to all men. Those who take part in it are variously implicated in the realities of the human city and it is up to them, in the light of the gospel, to assume those political positions to which their consciences prompt them. In other words, the word of God and the symbolical rites of the faith which constitute the essence of the liturgy transcend actual situations. It is up to Christians in each specific place and time in their temporal existence to influence political realities in accordance with their faith. When a worshipping assembly assumes a specific political connotation or orientation, that is accidental; and it is always injurious to the Church, which is not of itself linked with any particular politics.

But this mode of reasoning forgets that the liturgy, even before it is a proclaimed word and a celebrated rite, is first and foremost an assembly in the faith of actual men, an assembly at a certain time and a certain place, a fragment of the world, a part of the city of men. Rather than the word or the rite existing in themselves, the gospel cannot be proclaimed to the assembly in any other than *its* language and the paschal liberation cannot be celebrated by that assembly other than in *its* historic existence. The liturgy is not an accidental collection of individuals each listening to eternal truths and receiving in the sacrament an individual grace of salvation. It is a human group—a political reality—celebrating here and now the transition from slavery to liberty in the risen Christ, which cannot occur without an assault on the actual injustices of society, in order to win acceptance for other values.

Of course this practical a-political position of the liturgy implies a whole series of dichotomies (between eternity and time, the individual and society, the form and content of the message, the content and signifier of the sacrament, and so on), which are clearly incompatible with authentic Christian worship.

3. Well before Vatican II the contemporary pastoral liturgical renewal began to regret the a-temporal and uncommitted nature of a celebration whose formularies and rites connoted another age, other ways and other social structures. In addition, the post-conciliar reform of the liturgical books was primarily concerned to remove from formularies those expressions which had become incomprehensible or scandalous, then to put forward new texts which show the connection of the liturgical prayer with the realities of this world. The restoration of the prayer of the people is the most noteworthy element of this trend. To pray for the actual needs of the Church and the world is to show that one is intimately concerned with political realities, that the word and the sacrament point to the salvation of the world in which we live. The official books even provided Masses for various needs of the world: for example, for immigrants, social communications, and so forth. The Church's vision of and for the world expressed in *Gaudium et Spes* shows its influence on liturgical practice.

But does that mean that the internal political drive proper to liturgy has been liberated? I have shown that worship was concerned with the city of men—even to the extent sometimes of worrying or shocking some people. The faithful are being made conscious of their socio-political responsibilities. But does that mean that the celebration as such has become a more meaningful and effective mode of paschal liberation? I am not at all sure.[2]

Wishing to take into account the just complaint of Christians who thought that the liturgy was cut off from their real lives, those responsible for celebration introduced political themes. This accords with a pastoral emphasis which put the first weight of

[2] In regard to this point and many others in this essay I have benefited from unpublished notes by P. de Béthunes of Ottignies, Belgium, who is preparing a doctoral thesis on "Liturgy and Politics".

reform on the "contents" of the texts and liturgical rites, and which, in encouraging active participation, thought above all of "conscious" participation. But even if the referential aspect is essential to liturgical communication, it is not the only aspect and not always the most influential one. There are many others, known or unknown, which are often more important, for example everything emanating from the dynamic quality of the celebration and its inductive power. It is possible to have a celebration which has been strongly thematized by political realities and yet which has no influence on the life of the human city. In contrast, a liturgy without any political allusion can have so strong a political significance that the powers that be think it necessary to prohibit it, or try to make use of it.

When the liturgy is given a political theme without allowing the celebration to show its existential dynamics, the inadequacy is increased rather than reduced. The faithful are more indoctrinated than converted, and more convicted of guilt than liberated. "The annoyance one experiences at some celebrations presided over by a committed priest," de Béthunes writes, "is to a great extent attributable to the fact that such celebrations put forward a contestatory and progressivist theme ('You've got to commit yourselves, show some initiative, listen to the voice of the people'), while maintaining a dynamics of witness (a prefabricated liturgy; one that is directive, dominative, clerical). It is the liturgical language and not just its content which ought to be re-created by Christian communities."

4. The celebration which tries to be political but relies more on an ideology than on the paschal dynamics of the Christian mystery very soon becomes a politicized liturgy: that is, one used for specific political ends. "Whenever one uses theological discourse or the liturgical action in the service of an ideology drawn from elsewhere one is indulging in a form of manipulation contrary to their essential natures. Often with the best intentions, Christians commit such outrages when, for example, they try to impose on the liturgy a social message that it does not proclaim—even though, at the same time, they allow no sound of the liberating call proper to the liturgy. Unfortunately it is in this spirit that we are offered a number of so-called political liturgies which are in fact only superficially politicized and which try to compen-

sate the inadequacy of their political structure with an extreme theme ... they only succeed in moralizing and arousing a sense of guilt."

II. THE DYNAMICS OF A LIBERATING CELEBRATION

What can (and must) a group of Christians, members of the human city in which they are politically committed, expect from the celebration of the paschal mystery for their own liberation and that of the world?

Between the civic life of the members of the assembly and their liturgical action, there is a clear continuity. These are the same men, living one history, wishing to lead their lives in accordance with the gospel values in which they believe. But there is a no less obvious form of break: the liturgical action is of itself non-productive of immediate socio-political effects. Struggles for justice and for the liberation of the oppressed are effectively conducted otherwise. The celebration is a waste of time for effective initiative. Those on holiday are not at work. At the level of communion things are different. But what is the real efficacy of the celebration? And how is it apparent, for that which is proper to liturgy is visibly to signify the invisible, to make present that which is absent, and to bring about that which is not yet?

There is a dialectic of continuity-rupture-communion at the basis of liturgical dynamics. But the liturgy is practice rather than theory. It does not stop at the level of the -ologies (anthropology); theo- logy); it is concerned with the order of -urgies (liturgy). It is a symbolic action and an inductive force; it institutes a new existence. That is the way to look for its political power and liberating power.

The liturgy is a totalizing action: i.e., that which posits symbolically the intended term, the ultimate aim, the global meaning; which put it into practice by a form of ritual labour; at all levels it is the liberation of men by the re-born Christ which is at issue.

1. The overall reference

Celebration is the "assembly rejoicing" (Heb. 12. 22). The feast is the symbolical action where the group finds the meaning of its history. This symbolical action is a memorial. But Christian worship is not only a memorial of the past, it is also (and above all) a memory of the future. It is so because it only evokes the accomplishment of history—the term which makes sense: it realizes it. It re-presents, renders present the "last time"; the newness in the resurrected Christ where all creation "will be free from the slavery of corruption, in order to share in the freedom and glory of the children of God" (Rom. 8. 21).[3]

Each celebration is concerned not only with a specific political struggle; liberation in one place in the world and at one moment in history: it intends the total transformation of relations between God, man and the cosmos.

It is essential that the celebration should manifest this totality. But nowadays things don't happen of themselves. Already the effective exercise of memory is a difficult operation for our Western contemporaries who are imbued with an historicizing mentality in which the past is only a datable event or a reminiscence of a past reality. For the very young the future is suspect. Eschatological preoccupation has something about it of non-commitment, of refusal of the revolution. And our celebrations have great difficulty in signifying the present historic (the Bible is listened to as a story of another time), and even more the present future (the kingdom to come is received as an abstraction). However, if the celebration neglects to represent totality, any sense of actuality in the ritual symbols loses meaning. The symbols become useless (why do we still have Scripture and the sacraments?). The liturgical feast can also develop into a study circle, a political action meeting, the centre of a social and charitable action, a pious meeting offering the consolations of religion, and so on. Faced with the claim for a political dimension of liturgy, the Christian celebration cannot (lest it destroy itself) omit to signify the following three values.

(a) The group assembled here and now is more than itself. It is the *sacramentum* of the whole Church, of all the redeemed people (already free and not yet freed). Its paschal feast is the feast of all mankind in the dead and risen Christ. If that is not shown forth; if the liberating adventure of the liturgy is lived

---

[3] In regard to all this, see J. Moltmann's article in this issue.

only as that of the men united there: then it will be split-up among the faithful without the same socio-political objective.

(b) The word proclaimed is not an action programme but the "dangerous memory" of the sufferings of humanity as described by Metz, a permanent opposition to the powers that oppress mankind, a continual call to a personal and a collective conversion, the kerygma of liberation.[4] For that the moralizing, technological and ideological language which seemed more than anything plausible to our contemporaries (and which penetrates our celebrations) is inadequate. The liturgy has to use, among others, two modes of language: the narrative account (of the past and the future for today), whose importance for the faith and liturgy has been shown in two recent articles.[5] In many cases today these modes of language have to be learnt or re-learnt.

(c) The sacrament, especially that of the shared bread, is nothing if it is not an effective symbol for the faith of the kingdom to come. It does not give food to eat, like Oxfam, for starving nations, nor does it break the chains of prisoners. The kiss of peace or the penitential act does not *de facto* resolve all conflicts between members of the eucharistic assembly. They are mediated by an ongoing liberating process.

In order to celebrate politically, one has to be able to admit that the supreme politics is primarily the feast that makes us "live above our means" (H. Cox). It is the myth which tells of the unheard of; it is the Utopia which posits the impossible as necessary; it is the poetry which says that which is not there; it is the symbol which does that which is not done. It means admitting that the hour has not come to remove all ambiguities, because salvation is not won.

2. Ritual work

Nevertheless, we claim that our liturgy is not pure mythology, utopian symbolism, or a dream of hope. The celebration is for the men celebrating: for their true conversion and liberation, in the world where they live. Here we find in a practical way the exigencies of those who reject "uncommitted" worship, without

[4] See J. Llopis' article.
[5] H. Weinrich, "Narrative Theology", and J. B. Metz, "A Short Apology of Narrative", in *Concilium*, May 1973 (American edn., Vol. 85).

any "connection with their life", and this exigency should be met in so far as it is feasible.

In order to fulfil his promise in a non-mythic way, God entered into space and time. He made himself man in Jesus, the true history of liberation as the revealing *logos* and the saving *ergon*. The Christian faith and celebration has no other means. It is a location of criticism and work. It is not a form of work producing an object, but a ritual labour where man acts on himself and the group on itself in accordance with a model from the past.

Here we remember those legitimate current attempts to correct a liturgy in which nothing happens unless it be from above to below, without any real solidarity from the participants, without feedback, without any critical appeal within the group, or any circulation of sufferings borne or values hoped for. The celebration will show forth its political power only if the relations between the participants themselves constitute models which induce liberation. The following should be included among the manifestations of such relations.

(a) *The mutual welcome* by which the assembly constitutes itself is the first inductive sign of another mode of relations than that of the business world, of the world of parenthood or childhood, the club, and so on. Is this because anyone can welcome someone in the name alone of his confidence in the resurrected Christ? Is each individual received for himself, in positive respect for his "difference" of race, culture, political opinion, sex, age, social standing, degree of Christian initiation? All the ordinary links between force and power are already put in question if each man (including those ordained to the service of the assembly) is prepared to look upon every other as his brother and to consider him as superior to himself, as being for him Christ, a member of his Body. At the same time we should lose the anonymity of the crowd, the concealment of real differences, clerical power, and so on).

(b) *The circulation of the word* as the bearer of Christian hope is another ritual labour essential to the Christian liturgy. The reading of the Scripture and the presidential homily addressed to the assembly are perhaps not sufficient for the full circulation of the word. It seems today that Paul's precept, "Let the word of

Christ dwell in you richly in all wisdom; teaching and admonishing one another..." (Col. 3. 16), demands other means of communication. The word is not only the transmission of a divine message; it contains the answer that it evokes in the believing community. That also has to be communicated. Because there is not only one way of replying to the gospel challenge. The manifestation in the assembly of the complementary variety of responses of faith is an irreplaceable instance of criticism for Christian action, especially nowadays when the diversity of human situations sometimes reveals very different policies in practice, even though they are inspired by the same gospel.

(c) *The apportionment of intercession and the action of grace* constitute the community in the exercise of its priesthood between the world and God. He makes it an agent of paschal liberation.

The universal prayer of the people in the Mass is, for example, a privileged location of intercession. But we must attend, when formulating it, to its inductive model. To say "Let us pray to the Lord that war may cease in Vietnam" is ambiguous. This formula can be used in the assembly whether one is asking God to see to things, or one recognizes one's implication in this human sickness and so has suffered the result of the conflict. The form of the intercession can show the political force of the result of the conflict.

Similar thoughts are possible on prayers. The way in which an assembly formulates its prayer is particularly demonstrative of its political consciousness, while developing it and maintaining it.

To give thanks is to affirm that the liberating power of Christ risen is stronger than all the slaveries of this world. It is to acknowledge that it was so in the death and resurrection of Jesus, that it will be so definitively, but also that it is so effectively though partially for those who give thanks. It is important that the action of grace, the making of the eucharist, does not refer only to the historic past of Jesus and the eschatological future, but to the present paschal liberation. To proclaim its present signs in the liturgical assembly is necessary to the hope of those who fight for the justice of the kingdom.

I still have two points to make in regard to the ritual work of
the celebration as inductive of paschal liberation.

The first concerns the obvious fact that the liturgy functions
under the rule of signs and symbols. Even the work done remains
ritualistic. It is a transient action (every liturgical assembly is
destined to break up). The inductive dynamics of the liberating
rites does not concern the celebration as such but that to which
it directs: the life of Christians politically committed in the
world. In this sense, the rite is pre-political.

The second point concerns the functioning of the celebration.
The requests expressed here are more or less realizable according
to the size of the celebrating group. The very large group is above
all liable to show forth the feast and its global meaning. It can
hardly practise a mutual welcome or the effective imparting of
the word or of prayer, other than on its own symbolical level.
The contrary is true in a very small group where the commitment
of individuals may be expressed, but where the ecclesial significance is limited. These two types of assembly are useful and even
necessary. But they risk the long-term development of frustra-
tions among those who have no other opportunity of a celebration
(too big a Sunday assembly) or atrophy (sectarianism). In order
that the dynamics of a regular assembly can occur in an optimal
manner, in order to retain a feast and the accomplishment of
truly ritual process, an average number are needed (eighty to a
hundred and fifty individuals?). Beyond that (except for major
feastdays) there is the danger of falling into a functional witness, which is neutral, clerically hierarchized, and an invitation
to non-commitment in too weakly motivated believers.

III. Liberating Communion—New History

As a feastday assembly, the celebration shows forth the total
liberating project of God in the risen Christ. By its ritual work,
especially in confronting the reality of the world with the demands of the gospel, the assembled group commits itself his-
torically to the paschal venture. But this work and history are
not primarily those of the assembled faithful. It is God who saves.
It is the risen Christ who makes all things new. Man's
politics does not make the kingdom of God, but he makes his

kingdom come by means of those who welcome his justice and his love. More than the word which evokes the faith, the sacrament realizes the pact of the liberating covenant. In doing that, it relativizes all politic action by Christians by integrating it into the totality of salvation.

A liturgy of the word where the faithful have accepted the evangelical gospel challenge, and have acknowledged those oppressions of which they are victims, and for which they are at the same time responsible, can sometimes lead them to new communal decisions, to actual socio-political options. But in posing the gesture of communion to the liberated Body, their particular decisions and choices are situated into the total reality of salvation. They find themselves both validated and already opposed as inadequate. Because at the Lord's table there is also room for the passing stranger who is not directly concerned with the group choice, or the one who in conscience cannot accept it fully. The same communion welcomes those who cannot join fully. In the same communion there are those who have to struggle on other fronts according to different opinions. Finally, there are all those who have not come to the wedding feast.

It is important that any celebration should display at the same time the already inaugurated liberation, and the "not-yet" of universal salvation. It is the condition for which the liturgy not only opposes alien powers, but unceasingly contests the political commitment of Christians. The liturgy "proclaims this possible world which is the new Jerusalem, without any fear of evolving in the same celebration and by means of actualities which makes this ideal impossible. It is from the shock encounter of this *impossible* with this *possible* that there awakens a call to go beyond fatalism with the Spirit of the Resurrected. . . . It is above all in celebrating the mystery of our liberation in Christ that we are led to oppose all that which alienates, all that which prevents men (and us first) from being really themselves, of achievement in God, but without rushing through the stages which lead from liberation from misery, by way of the rediscovery of dignity, the resumption of initiative, to the recognition of supreme values and a life consciously received from God and shared with others. For this liberation is no longer absolute. Confronted by a secularist ideal which recommends a total and individualist independence, a sort of social weightlessness, the political liturgy hymns with Miriam, the transition from slavery to service" (P. de Béthunes).

IV. CONCLUSION

Between those today in the Church who show no interest in the liturgy because it seems to have no connection with their evangelical commitment to the world, and those who on the contrary use the liturgy as the ideological and practical contribution of a specific political orientation, the celebration, as the feast of paschal liberation, brings Christians something indispensable they will not find elsewhere.

(a) Theological talk as well as pastoral orientations are necessary to the life of the Church. But the one and the other are perforce subject to ideological and contingent determinations. The ritual language of the liturgy, though assuredly more ambiguous, is also more open. The symbol, the narrative, the feast always escape logical reductions and those of planning. They are a set of permanent ironical comments on our thought and planning.

(b) In the statutes of a Church still largely connected, in many places, with the dominant power, the celebration is the chance to allow the emergence of the alternative, Utopia, eschatology, without paying them any special attention.

(c) When religious language is de-structured to the point where all valid discourse about God and Christ seems in certain respects impossible.

The saving economy of an hermeneutics need not (and must not) be practised. But it is no longer a necessary preliminary. The living man is primarily the one who plays and celebrates.

Translated by V. Green

PART II
BULLETIN

Herman Schmidt

Political Symbols, Poems and Songs

BECAUSE symbols, poetry and song have an essential place in liturgical celebrations it seems useful to think about politics in connection with liturgy, since the same kind of thing is found in both. Symbols such as banners, escutcheons, emblems and images, abbreviations, ceremonies, have a considerable role to play in politics (Section I). In every country, the national anthem is a symbol of mutual solidarity (II). Spirituals, "seculars" and blues are expressions of humanity reflecting the experiences of the American negro, whose life has been one of slavery and who is in process of freeing himself from political oppression (III). In our own age with its political, social and economic unrest, many people are not happy about the world and its ways and poems and songs of protest, resistance and revolution are found everywhere (IV). We are faced here with areas that are rich in material but to which little or no attention has been paid in theology and the science of liturgy. That is why I will concentrate on these subjects and will offer for inspection some of the many political symbols, poems and songs found at present in the world.

I. POLITICAL SYMBOLS

An attempt to document political symbols cannot start from a theological, philosophical or liturgical theory of symbolism. It is not just in those three areas that symbols have a major role, but in cultures, in the pictorial arts, languages, politics, mathematics, chemistry, the physical sciences, in short, the whole range of day-to-day life. Where the study of liturgy is concerned, it is useful and even necessary to know something about symbols and symbolism in other areas.

There are many reasons for this. To assert, for instance, that for modern man symbols constitute a "blind spot" is an unacceptable generalization, if it stems from a conviction that people no more have feeling for *liturgical* symbols. The truth is that a general insensitivity to symbols is only a fact if it registers in all areas. What is more, the lack of a feeling for liturgical symbols, where it exists, can be attributed to two things: namely, a blunting of liturgical sensitivity in people or sclerosis of the symbolism found in liturgy.

There is a scarcity of literature on modern political symbolism. One can find specialized information on the subject in the annual publications of the heraldic society *Zum Kleeblatt* in Hanover (from 1965 onwards), in the *Flag Bulletin* of the Flag Research Center at Lexington (Mass.) and scattered about here and there in various other inaccessible publications. Arnold Rabbow has opened up this territory for a wider public in the copiously illustrated *dtv-Lexikon politischer Symbole* (Munich, 1970).[1]

In the realm of politics, symbols are a means of communication between people and play a major role alongside verbal and pictorial modes of intercourse. A symbol is a thing that stands for something else and evokes it. Man sees the reality that faces him not just as something physical, but also and more particularly as an expression of and pointer to realities within the human mind and spirit. A symbol is a compressed expression of highly charged and many-sided meaning. Political symbols enshrine political ideals, pretensions to power, standards and demands, declarations of war, even total views of the world and ideologies; and these they transpose into a single image or token. For anyone familiar with the mental and intellectual background to such

---

[1] A lot of symbols used in the political sphere one comes across in other places too, but often with a different range of meanings. This is especially true of the Bible and iconography. See, e.g., Manfred Lurker, *Wörterbuch biblischer Bilder und Symbole* (Munich, 1973); J. Timmers, *Symboliek en iconographie der christelijke kunst* (Roermond and Maaseik, 1947).

symbols they evoke associations and reactions, assent or repudiation.

The written language has not supplanted the language of symbols, because a symbol or image goes beyond the boundaries of language. Modern scientific disciplines and movements make use of signs and symbols which not only dispense information around the world but also stir people into action—for example, mathematical and technical signs, traffic signs, advertising, medical symbols, and so on. In theology, philosophy and liturgical science some writers deny to these modern signs and tokens the status of symbols, because they are held to provide nothing more than information and are not *signum efficax*. As I see it, this ignores the fact that such signs do not furnish us with unbiased, "neutral" information, but through their colours, shapes and representational character arouse men to human and often morally necessary activity.

So far as the liturgy of Vatican II is concerned, the complaint one hears is that it is too verbal and devoid of symbolic power. Symbolism has to be seen as a totality of symbols and signs; to restrict oneself to "essential" or "sacramental" symbols smacks of rationalism. "Essential" and "sacramental" symbols are really sufficient when interwoven with suitable "accessory" symbols; for they are then in their proper setting. Where that is not the case they are left hanging in a void (the minimum required for the validity of a sacrament) or are smothered in an unsuitable atmosphere (a sacrament immersed in an excess of didactics, commentary, moralizing and theoretical chit-chat). In my view this digression is in place here because the strength of political symbolism is quite possibly underestimated and that of liturgical symbolism in one sense (rationalistically) overestimated. Now that the vernacular languages have displaced a universal but unintelligible Latin, the symbolism that transcends language barriers and so can be understood everywhere deserves special consideration in a religion which is itself catholic and universal.

To give the reader an idea of political symbols the most important are listed and briefly described below.

1. Banners were in use in olden times as battle-emblems and standards, feudal and seignorial symbols, the distinguishing marks of guilds or associations (e.g., bands of musicians) and as

symbols of various religious manifestations (e.g., the banners of the saints). Showing the flag started at the beginning of the seventeenth century as a means of communicating by colours in navigation. Regions, provinces and cities too employ flags as symbols and with the growth of nationalism each nation eventually came to adopt a flag of its own. The national flags consist of colour-symbols with or without emblematic symbols, which have particular meanings of their own in each country. Most had their origin in a struggle for liberation, a revolution, a declaration of independence. In all nations the national flag is an especially powerful symbol of unity and nationalism. No smear must be cast upon it, because it is "sacral". Although most of the people know neither the flag's history nor the significance of the colours and emblems, yet it serves to indicate a lofty value: the national consciousness and national pride. Military forces and those who wield political power are most conversant with the national colours and are united around them.

2. Coats of arms are shields (escutcheons) that carry symbolical signs and tokens meant to distinguish (noble) families, cities, regions, provinces, states, nations, international institutions. They are a sort of duplicate of the flags. Because they appear on shields and so do not flap about in the wind, they can combine a multiplicity of colours and emblems into a symbolic whole and attach to them a succinctly worded motto. Heraldry is concerned with the history, laws and designing of coats of arms. These first appeared in the twelfth century at the time of the Crusades and were originally military insignia. Although found on innumerable buildings, inside and outside, and on every conceivable object, they are even less well known to ordinary people and are therefore mainly of interest to the individuals and institutions directly concerned. Their symbolism is usually so complicated that it calls for both explanation and a degree of specialist knowledge.

3. An enormous number of objects, shapes and pictorial representations, more especially from the realm of botany and fauna, are found in political symbolism. This practice had its beginning in a distant past before an alphabetical script had been invented and people used picture-writing, vestiges of which can still be found in very ancient languages and among primitive

peoples. One can still see pictorial emblems of this sort on flags and especially on coats of arms. Most favoured are the eagle, the lion, the dragon and the cock in every conceivable shape. Younger nations have introduced new animals: for instance, the bull (Bechuanaland), the elephant (Ivory Coast, Guinea), the croco- dile (Lesotho) and the rhinoceros (Sudan). Even in everyday life people recognize each other very well in animals and . . . brute beasts. Where plants are concerned we have wreaths or garlands of palms, laurels and ears of corn, not to mention trees and some- times flowers (the French lily). Sun, moon (half moon) and stars occur in every kind of form. Then again, we find tools, weapons (lances, arrows, swords) and abstract or geometrical figures. From Christianity there have worked their way into political symbolism, in particular, the cross (specifically, the cross of St Andrew in Scotland, the cross of St George in England, the cross of Jerusa- lem in the period of the Crusades, the Lotharingian cross) and on occasion the Christ-monogram and the dove (of peace).

4. Because political symbols have a considerable influence on the formation of public opinion, they are admirably suited to the purposes of propaganda and persuasion. That is true of all poli- tical systems, but it is a striking fact that totalitarian ideologies or movements and dictatorial power-systems in particular— whether of the right (fascism, Nazism) or of the left (com- munism)—make a more intensive use of the political symbol than do parliamentary democracies and middle-of-the-road parties and groups. In the twentieth century, the political symbol has developed into an efficient means of canvassing or manipu- lating the masses and the stress is now on power, on influencing and dominating the masses, socially and economically weak as they are, in order to defeat the capitalist systems by violence and revolution and to reward the labour of the economically de- pressed classes. The most potent symbol of communism is the colour red, particularly the red flag and the red star, the hammer and sickle, the clenched fist. In the case of fascism, typical features are the fasces, the colour black, the raised and outstretched arm, in Nazism, the swastika and the colour brown, and in Falangism, the yoke and arrows and the colour blue.

5. Symbols of modern international organizations and move- ments have less success, as for instance the anti-atomic weapon

symbol, the Atomium of the 1958 World Exhibition in Brussels (a symbol of technical development and co-operation), the Benelux flag (Belgium, Luxembourg and The Netherlands), the green E of the European movement. In South Asia, especially in South Vietnam, the Buddhists' flag is well known as the symbol of a political movement, and all over the world the Olympic flag with its five rings. During the Second World War the V-sign (made with the index- and middle fingers) enjoyed great success.

6. Much in vogue at present are abbreviations of a word or of several words together. They are used primarily to designate political parties. International institutions and movements too are often denoted by an abbreviation; but this sometimes creates confusion, as the shortened forms can occur in many different languages. NATO (the North Atlantic Treaty Organization) also has an emblem and UNO (the United Nations Organization) has a symbol.

7. Political functions and celebrations are conducted according to a protocol of ceremonies at the installation of heads of state, military ceremonies, parades, funerals, dedication ceremonies for youth (in communist countries), admittance to associations and secret societies, and so forth. Clothing too plays an important role, for example, with the army, state officialdom, the judiciary, youth movements, revolutionary and anarchist organizations. Headgear—crown, cap, and so on—is important too. Then, finally, it is worth remembering postage-stamps in connection with political symbols, especially because they are so popular.

II. NATIONAL ANTHEMS

In every nation, the national song or anthem is the most expressive symbol of mutual solidarity. Because it is an audiovisual thing, everyone can give personal and active expression to his patriotic feelings by joining in the singing of the anthem, of which he will know the first familiar verse or so, at any rate, even in his sleep. At official (especially military) gatherings, and when foreign heads of state are being welcomed, a band plays the tune of the guest's national anthem and then that of the home country, while everyone keeps reverentially silent and the military salute. Anybody who remains demonstrably indifferent or adopts an attitude of protest shows a lack of patriotism or is staging an objection to the policies of his own country or to the *force majeure* exercised by a foreign nation or colonizing people.

A critical collection of all national anthems has been published by the German Institute for Foreign Relations: *Die National-hymnen der Erde* (Munich). The same institute has published an extract of the above-mentioned work: *Nationalhymnen; Texte und Melodien* (Stuttgart, 1972). Both editions give the original texts with a German translation and the tunes.

1. Many national anthems perpetuate the memory of liberation from foreign overlords through war and revolt or of domestic peace achieved after bloody revolutions. In Europe, one can read from the national anthems how the nations came into existence. In the United States of America, the national anthem refers rather to the unification of the various states and above all to the welding together of people coming from every state one could think of, and now united in a supra-national alliance in which the emphasis is not on nationalism (as in Europe) but on Americanism. In a way, the word "national" becomes a neutral, purely practical concept there, so that "nationalism" in the sense of "affectionate attachment to a nation" might perhaps be better described as "patriotism": an enthusiasm for the "Fathers" (*Patres*) who, coming from all over the world, have bonded themselves together in the new world after a great deal of struggle and strife and readjustment.[2] In Central and South America, Africa, Asia and Oceania, most national anthems, having emerged after some declaration of independence, testify to a victory over colonialism. Although there are some such anthems that strike a bloodthirsty note, most of them put the accent on freedom and peace, finally achieved after much sacrifice, misery and bloodshed.

2. Not just in nations which have not been through any bloody wars of liberation, but in others too the national anthems celebrate the beauty and wealth of the country. Nature especially is extolled and idealized. The Austrian sings of his fatherland as: "Land of mountains, land on the river, land of fields, land of cathedrals". The Swedes sing of: "The sweetest land on earth".

---

[2] As regards bibliography see also the article *Nationalismus* in Helmut Schoeck, *Kleines soziologisches Wörterbuch* (Freiburg, 1969).

The Chileans exclaim: "Your country, bordered with flowers, is the happy likeness of Eden". The Dane starts with: "I know a glorious land" and has the nerve to sing about its handsome girls.

3. When it comes to the young nations of Africa, the words of their national anthems are conspicuous for their peaceful character. The dominant theme is "to work". In 1972, the song entitled *La Zaïrose* (words by Simon-Pierre Boka, music by Joseph Lutumba) was officially declared to be the national anthem of Zaire:

> Zairans, we have peace once more,
> A united people, Zairans are we.
> Forward, proud and full of dignity,
> A great people, a free people for ever.
>
> Tricolour, kindle in us the holy fire
> To build our country, ever more splendid,
> Around a "River-Majesty",
> Around a "River-Majesty".
>
> Tricolour, in the wind, revive the ideal,
> That binds us to our forefathers, to our children;
> PEACE, JUSTICE AND WORK,
> PEACE, JUSTICE AND WORK.

4. Religious themes are worked into a number of national songs. That of Iceland is a prayer:

> O, God of our country! O, country of our God!
> Your name is sacred to us, yes, sacred every moment.
> Galaxy upon galaxy, bound to you by the ages,
> Weaves for you a garland, out of the solar systems.
> For you a day is a thousand years
> And a thousand years are but a day.
> A trembling flower, that in humility
> Raises its tiny head
> To greet you, and then perishes:
> Iceland's thousand years, Iceland's thousand years:
> A trembling little bloom.

The British national anthem is also a prayer: "God save the Queen". The Iranians sing: "Iranians have been happily united, God is their protector". And in Malta: "Protect, O Lord, as always, this native land of ours that has given us a name. Forget it not, for you made it so beautiful". Or: "Guard her, O Lord, as ever Thou hast guarded, this Motherland so dear whose name we bear". Sometimes the homeland is treated as divine, God's blessing is invoked upon armaments, God's vengeance called down upon enemies.

5. Music plays a major role, because quite often the words are not sung. Several national anthems have preserved ancient melodies: for instance, Brazil has a song from the sixteenth century: "Deutschland, Deutschland über alles" preserves a melody from Haydn's 1797 "Kaiser Quartet" (op. 76, nr. 3); the Dutch anthem is a version of a French song by Valerius van Veere (1626); the Austrian has a melody from Mozart's minor "Freemason's Cantata" of 1791. A gramophone record (OCORA OCR 31) contains the music (without words) of the national anthems of nineteen young African nations.

III. Spirituals, Seculars and Blues

1. *Bibliographical guide*. "Folk music" is something found all over the world. Every people has something distinctive in its songs and instrumental music, which as time goes on is conserved and yet also developed. In the case of nations who because of their long-standing contacts with one another produce music of an international kind, their folk songs and instrumental folk music are usually distinguished as "popular music" from aesthetic "serious" or "classical" music as well as from "light music", so called. In dealing with this, that and the other nation, historians of music set out to discover the original forms of the popular music that has come down to us; and so we talk about popular music and primitive music. A general and well-documented study is the one by Roberto Leydi, *Musica popolare e musica primitiva; Guida breve alla conoscenza degli stili spontanei* (Turin, 1959) with an extensive bibliography in the notes and with a discography in the appendix (pp. 253–89).

The bibliography on the music of the North American negro

is very extensive. For our purpose we can refer the reader to, for instance, two books by Lothar Zenetti: *Peitsche und Psalm; Geschichte und Glaube, Spirituals und Gospelsongs der Neger Nordamerikas* (Munich, ²1967), with a discography, table of literature, list of sources and indexes (pp. 246–72) and *Heisse (W)eisen; Jazz, Spirituals und Schlager in der Kirche* (Munich, 1966). In *Concilium,* February 1969 (American edn., Vol. 42), information is to be found in Helmut Hucke's bulletin, "Jazz and Folk Music in the Liturgy", and in *Concilium,* November 1970 (American edn., Vol. 59), Theodor Lehmann's bulletin, "A Cry of Hope: the Negro Spirituals".

One can get some understanding of how Spirituals have developed, if for instance one makes a comparison between the following records: Atlantic (SD 1351) (Southern Folk Heritage Series ST-A-60 277/8): (1) *Negro Church Music*, recorded in the field and edited by Alan Lomax assisted by Shirley Collins; (2) Tribute Record (TR-103): *A Mountain Mass and Folk Songs from the Mountains* (The Western Carolina Singers); (3) London American Recordings (LDY 379 254): *The Voices of Victory*, a service by the pastor and the choir of the Victory Baptist Church, Los Angeles, California; (4) Pro Civitate Christiana (PCC CS 0150): *The Folkstudio Singers; A man called Jesus*, edited by Eddie Hawkins; (5) Pro Civitate Christiana (PCC CS 0152): *The Folkstudio Singers; Bethlehem City of Light*, edited by Eddie Hawkins; (6) Pro Civitate Christiana (PCC CS 0153): *Deep River*, a recital by Don Powell.

James H. Cone, *The Spirituals and the Blues; an Interpretation* (New York, 1972), is an important book on politics and liturgy. This title given to the German translation is something that Cone said of himself: "I am the Blues and my life is a Spiritual" and there is a Foreword by Jürgen Moltmann. Prior to this book, Cone wrote two theological studies, both very startling and bewildering for the white reader, *Black Theology and Black Power* (New York, 1969) and *A Black Theology of Liberation* (New York, 1970). He presents a "black theology", which gives full weight to the concrete situation and the struggle of the black community, and a "theology of liberation", projected in and with the people, out of the suffering of alienation towards a praxis of liberation. At the world missionary conference in Bangkok in January 1973, black theology came up for discussion apropos of problems concerning Christianity and racial discrimination. In a lot of countries, being a Christian means awaking out of political subjugation and racial estrangement. In other countries, being Christian means stirring oneself out of complicity in the oppression and out of alienation from other races and peoples. Thus in Latin America we find a "theology of liberation" and in Africa a peculiarly African theology. The concrete starting-point is as diverse as the situations are. In common they remember the poor, oppressed, crucified Christ and hope in that kingdom of freedom in which he rose from the dead for us.

2. Black theology in America also has as sources and acts of testimony the songs of the negroes, once sold in Africa by their fellow tribesmen and the Muslims to the British, French, Dutch, Portuguese and Spaniards, who carried them off to America, where they were bought as slaves by whites who had immigrated there from every part of Europe. In these songs, a nation of slaves, a herd made by human beings, a herd of human beings, reduced to animals, gives expression to its experiences—a nostalgic longing for Africa, suffering and oppression, hope for deliverance and freedom, disillusion after a liberation that is no freedom at all.

In our own time, these songs are popular all over the world. In whites they stir up a consciousness of guilt and among Christions their Judas-like treachery. They are the resonance of the experience of a new slavery that afflicts many, both in their society from the power of capital, the economy, politics and prosperity and in their churches, where alien forces and influences hold Christian freedom in bonds. One does not need to be a Jew to cry out to God with the psalms of the Old Testament, to yearn with them after a lost Jerusalem, to sing them as an expression of one's own faith. It is not necessary to be black oneself to sing "Deep River", "Go down Moses", "O freedom, freedom over me". These songs rudely awaken the bad conscience of white people and take them up into the all-embracing liberation-movement of God.

It was impossible for the negroes in America to keep their own African religious traditions intact, because they had been totally uprooted and mixed together in a quite arbitrary way. Christianity they encountered among their white owners, not in their conduct but in the religious exercises (or liturgy) which as slaves they were compelled to attend, and in the observance of Christian festivals. They received from Christianity a variety of Bible stories which found a fruitful soil in their primal religious feelings and in their experiences of slavery.

What emerged was a new form of Christianity, a marvellous amalgam of primitive religiosity, exasperating bondage and biblical stories of redemption. They instinctively rejected the Christianity of their white masters, with their churches and missionaries, while letting it pass over their heads. Baptism did indeed make a Christian of the negro, but did not set him free. Under the law negroes were persons, yet also property. Their masters were adept at making devoted slaves of them. They were trained on Christian lines in so far as that was of use in fitting them for honest service, slavish subjection and faithful labour. But at the same time they reached through to the heart of Christianity by way of the biblical stories which they heard over and over again and cherished deep within their hearts.

A man must narrate in order to become himself. This self comes about in the first instance by listening to the many stories that are told and secondly by relating how a man has become what he is. There is a difference between talking about God and living with stories about Yahweh: "I-am-there". There are a lot of powerful stories in the Bible which arouse wonder and inspire us. Jesus of Nazareth was a speaker who above all used the story-form. From the time of Jesus' death not only have his own sayings been passed on but, whatever may be told about Jesus, stories of one who was dead and is alive. Jesus not only spoke in parables but in his whole ministry is the living parable of God, a parable which again and again faces readers of the gospel with the choice —to be for him or against him. The negro slaves were all the time trying to find in the old stories respite and recuperation.[3] The biblical stories of exile and bondage, deliverance and justice, hope and love, happiness and a future, they interpreted in their

[3] See "Leven met verhalen", *Schrift*, 26 (1973), pp. 41–77; H. Weinrich, "Narrative Theology", and J. Metz, "A Short Apology of Narrative", *Concilium*, May 1973 (American edn., Vol. 85).

songs, which they would sing together as they worked, in the late evening and on their non-working days, called by the whites Sundays and festivals.

These songs have acquired the splendid name of spirituals because they set slaves free, spiritually, and induced in them a kind of euphoric mood in which they could escape from harsh realities. The songs helped to create for them another world, the idea of a future, and made it possible to put up with the way things actually were. The spirituals are like a breath of freedom to a man, a succession of longings, constantly reiterated, a cry of lamentation and at the same time of jubilation. They are community songs for soloist, chorus and the many voices of the crowd. In the spirituals inspired by the Bible, the negroes are able to tell each other what they are doing in the land of bondage to stick by one another and keep their end up. It is said of the people of Israel that they could not sing the Lord's song in a strange land. But the negroes were able to sing in the strange land because their very being was the song and to sing was their very life. The spirituals enabled them to preserve their African identity amid the American slavery and gave them the rhythm to cope with their situation and come through. The "Africanism" in the spirituals is of a piece with the functional character of African music, which is an expression and experience of day-to-day living, working and playing.

In the spirituals, the black slaves combine reminiscence of their forebears with the Christian gospel and created a life-style through which they themselves contributed to their liberation from earthly slavery. Their bodies were taken from them and made the property of white people, but their spirit remained their own and, as they sang and sang in unending repetition, became infused with the Spirit of God living in the suffering and risen Christ. The spiritual is a spirituality of life in an extreme of misery and total ruin, lived out in the Man of Sorrows and his stricken people. The spiritual looks misery straight in the face—man is sorrowful, not knowing where to go, socially, economically and politically powerless, but not spiritually destroyed, so that he can sing: "I'm not wearied yet". This experience of distress does not become a weariness with life, a total apathy, self-destruction, but a joyous experience, a saying "yes" to life.

The spiritual is community in rhythm, dancing together in the movement of living. There *is* redemption, and ultimately resurrection in the risen Lord, whose life no man can take from him, despite the lash, the cross and the grave. Black history is itself a spiritual.

3. Of course there was negative reaction to the spiritual as well. Not every slave was able to find courage and strength to endure in the sense of religion he had brought with him from Africa and in the biblical stories. Some became sarcastic and embittered in their misery. Again it was in song that they expressed their impotence, cynicism and pessimism. Because such songs are non-religious and at times anti-religious, they are known as "seculars", in contrast to the spirituals. The religiously motivated population, including the majority of negroes, repudiated these songs and called them "devil's songs". The secular is aimed at the religious belief of the whites, which it cannot take seriously in any respect. Viewed against that background, it is understandable that they should ridicule the biblical stories, in particular the creation, the fall of man, the Flood. "Reign, Lord Jesus, reign" becomes "Rain, Lord, make it rain! Rain down flour and fat in my back-yard, with a big pigshead as well." And after a hard period of corrective discipline and punishment the despairing victim might sing: "O, poor devil, you, you'll be free, sure enough, when the good Lord sets you free". The seculars are not in a strictly philosophical sense atheistic. They leave God out of the picture and restrict themselves to the difficulties and troubles which the slaves could do nothing about and they apply white categories to the insurmountable situation of oppression. In a word, they are a parody.

4. After the emancipation of the negroes come the "blues". Liberation from slavery gave the negroes a certain feeling of autonomy and self-awareness. They could move around freely, be alone and reflect, develop themselves intellectually and take decisions, get together and organize themselves. But at the same time they found that freedom could also be burdensome. As slaves they had been safe inside a social system. As slaves they had shelter, clothing, food, protection. They could satisfy their sexual urges in the service of their masters' slave-rearing. But once free, they were on their own and had to make every next

move themselves. They had never learnt to depend on themselves for getting work, to earn money, to look after a house, obtain their own clothing and food and live as sexually responsible human beings. "There used to be no call for me to have any money, and now everybody asks me whether I have any." Another factor was that the whites left them to their fate and refused to accept them as fully responsible citizens. Their liberty was a contradiction, a caricature. They were equal to the whites and yet cut off from them, with equal rights under the law, in principle, but excluded from white society and without political influence. They were free, but second-class citizens. They were forced to wage a new battle against discrimination and the ghetto, a battle that has not altogether been fought and won, even now.

A new experience came their way: "A negro can never become a white man". In a sense, he could never fully share in the dominant level of the white man's culture. Hence being black and staying black became for him a value and a mission. He went on singing his spirituals and at the intersection of black and white also began to sing new songs of joy and sorrow, love and hate, and of the fearsome burden for the negro of being "free" in a society built on racial discrimination. Thus the blues emerged alongside the Christian spiritual, not as formerly songs for everyone to sing together but solos sung by prophets, interpreting their own experiences of suffering, love, sexuality, protest and hope, for an audience that can recognize itself in the singer and will let him stir it up to self-affirmation and the winning of real freedom. The blues-singer Henry Townsend from St Louis said: "When I'm singing the blues, I'm singing the truth" (not "I'm singing about the truth", or as James Cone says: "I am the blues". The blues are true in that they unite, they bind together, art and life, poetry and experience, the symbolic and the real. They form a response of artistry to the chaos of living. The blues give concrete, immediate and emotional expression to all of life's experiences; they are living art. One could call them a personification of the most private feelings and experiences of the black man. The "blues-person" is no alien being but someone the negro knows intimately. "When I woke up early today, the blues was shuffling around my bed. I sat down to breakfast and there was the blues in the bread. And I said: Mornin', blues. How y'doin', blues? Yeah, blues, how y'doin'? Me, I'm fine. Good mornin'. How are yer?" In whatever circumstances the negroes of America feel themselves to be negroes, through and through, both children of God (spirituals) and children not of animals but of human beings (blues).

IV. MODERN POLITICAL POEMS AND SONGS

Since the Second World War, mankind has been in a state of social, economic and political unrest and, despite the "economic miracle", there is injustice and oppression, pain and misery, not only in the Third World, so called, but also in the inner suburbs and slums of the industrial centres of the rich West. As in the past, man the under-dog gives expression in protest-songs to his day-to-day experience of the struggle for sheer life. The men in power fear such protests; and where they can act dictatorially they forbid the songs and render their poets and musicians harmless by sending them into exile or to gaol. But still a lot of protest songs are well known and are brought out in print, on disc and on tape. Thus there is a large but unmanageable spread of informative material, which it is not easy to get hold of and arrange in some sort of pattern. There are very few bookshops and discotheques specializing in this particular genre.[4] The documentation here will be confined to a few outstanding publications that reveal something of what protest songs are all about.

1. For pedagogical purposes, Wilhelm Gössmann has edited *Protestieren—Nachdenken—Meditieren—Beten*; Texte für den Schulgebrauch; Ausgabe A: Texte, Kommentar, Unterrichtsentwürfe (Für die Hand des Lehrers) (Werkbuch 90); Ausgabe B: Texte (Für die Hand des Schülers) (Werkbuch 91), Munich, 1970, and Günter Betz, *Politische Gedichten*; Für die Schule ausgewählt und erläutert (Werkbuch 92), Munich, 1970.

2. As far as Europe is concerned we shall confine ourselves to a few particulars to do with Russia and Italy.

Bruno Carnevali provides an anthology of *Blok—Esenin—*

---

[4] An enormous collection of discs and tape-recordings of protest-songs may be found in the *Rinascita* bookshop and discotheque in Rome.

Majakovski—Pasternak; poeti russi nella rivoluzione (Rome, 1971). The collection starts with a lengthy introduction and gives bio- and bibliographical particulars of each poet; the poems are presented in Russian with an Italian translation. An unpretentious little book is *La preghiera di Solzenicyn e il paradosso delle voci clandestine* (Milan, ²1971). It is published by the Centro Studi "Russia Cristiana" in Milan. The poems are given in an Italian translation alone. They have been brought together from official Russian literary journals and the independent press, the Samizdat, to which belong also the clandestine periodicals Sfinksy, Sintaksis, Feniks, etc. Many records of the Soviet Army choirs under Boris Alexandrov are available containing popular Russian songs.

In Italy, where as is well known the communist party is, after Russia, the strongest in Europe, there is a collection called *Canzoniere della protesta* (Milan, 1972). It gives 50 songs, text and music, and with them reprints of posters and pamphlets, and a discography. A simple textual edition of various revolutionary songs is *Se il vento fischiava* (Rome, 1973). The quality of these texts and songs leaves something to be desired. The communist party is planning to issue more such collections. In the Italian edition of IDOC Internazionale 4 (1973) 9–20, under the title *La canzone politica di protesta*, two anthologies with commentary have been published: Giovanna Marini, *La cultura popolare come mezzo di lotta*, and Maria Lucia Pereira, *Dai canti negri alla bossa-nova politica*.

3. Well known everywhere are the "psalms" of Ernesto Cardenal from Nicaragua: *Salmos* (Medellín, 1964, and Ávila, 1967). Interesting are the titles of some of the translations: German, *Zerschneide den Stacheldraht* (Wuppertal, 1967); French, *Cri, psaumes politiques* (Terres de feu) (Paris); Italian, *Grido; Salmi degli oppressi* (Assisi, 1971); Netherlands, *Protest achter prikkeldraad* (Amsterdam, ²1968). There are editions also in Argentina, Chile, Colombia, Denmark, Britain, Norway, Venezuela, the United States and Sweden. J. Buskes says of these psalms: "Cardenal identifies me with the man who in the Old Testament psalms prays to God, fights with God, defies God, doubts God, has faith in God, is afflicted by God and yet praises God, gives tongue to his despair and his hope in God's presence, begs God

to succour the oppressed and reward the oppressors. From the injustice done to people he does not infer the death of God, but from out of the death of a sick society he cries out to the living God and asks Him to vindicate the oppressed."

One can immediately sense the revolutionary history of Latin America running right through the song in the publication *Basta!* (Paris, 1967, and Milan, 1970), a detailed account of 182 protest-songs with original and translated text and a tape recording of 29 songs. There is no introduction, but each song is described in detail and is thus set in the concrete situation of the singers. The publication is arranged not by country, but on the basis of thirteen themes that come out in the songs. Most of the words are fiercely hostile to the established political and ecclesiastical order. Only by listening with the closest attention to what the tapes are really saying can one get to the very heart of the song—harsh words then become sad words, unbelief reveals a covert faith, in the despair hope is not wholly stifled, in the hate there is a love of justice and freedom.

Stefan Baciu and Kurt Marti have edited poems between revolution and Christianity from sixteen Latin American countries, under the title *Der Du bist im Exil* (Wuppertal and Barmen, 1969). They are presented in a German translation without introduction and commentary. In a postscript (pp. 135–8) Kurt Marti recognizes the weakness of this collection, presenting as it does whatever could be got hold of quite uncritically. "The problem of violence and non-violence is the social-cum-ethical framework of the tension between revolution and Christian belief. What the collection offers is not this or that theological and socio-ethical pronouncement but poems. In them revolution and belief are reflected in every possible nuance of human feeling, thinking, hoping—and that without ideological fixations. We listen not to any doctrines or theses (or if we do, of a subjective kind only), but to individual voices and testimonies—asseverations of hope, of despair, lostness, dismay (at what goes on), reflection after the event, complainings, love. Faith in these poems is no cloistered, bookish piety: blasphemy next to praise, nadaistic and other forms of nihilism next to prayers, litanies side by side with execration. Often the opposites are inseparably linked together. This anthology, therefore, proclaims no rigidly circumscribed ideo-

logy, whether revolutionary or Christian. Nor have these poems a
uniform literary style—on the contrary, from diffuse rhetoric to
succinct, even compact, condensation, from artifice to the fron-
tiers of *Kitsch* (or should it be Pop-art?) there is a little bit of
everything present and represented here."

4. There are anthologies made up of poems and songs from
the Portuguese colonies of Angola, Mozambique, Cape Verde
Islands, Guinea-Bissau and São Tomé: for instance, an extensive
one by Giuseppe Tavani, *Poesia africana di rivolta* (Bari, 1969)
(Portuguese text with Italian translation) and a smaller one by
Bertus Dijk, *Vuur en ritme* (Nesserie) (Amsterdam, 1969) (Dutch
translation only). As regards the authors (most of them natives)
these collections refer us to the sources, usually published outside
Portugal. From this moving literature we give here a poem by
José Craveirinha, born in 1922 at Lourenço Marques (Mozambique):

The Cry of the Negro

I am coal from the pit!
And you tear me out of the ground
and make me your mine, boss.

I am coal from the pit!
And you ignite me, boss,
to serve you as a motive force for ever
but not for ever, boss.

I am coal from the pit
and must burn, yes,
burn everything with the strength of my incineration.

I am coal from the pit
I must blaze under exploitation
blaze alive like tar, my brother
Till I am no longer your mine, boss.

I am coal from the pit
I must blaze
must burn up everything with the fire of my combustion.

Yes!
I'll be your coal, boss!

We are informed about Mozambique's struggle for freedom on a record (W F 01, Grafiche Dotti–Cernobbio) *W FRELIMO; documenti e canti del popolo Mozambicano in lotta contro il colonialismo Portoghese*. The sleeve sets out in chronological order the principal events between 1447 and 1972 and a brief documentation on the country as it is today. The disc is a collage-montage of drum music, dances, political songs and declamation in Italian of revolutionary texts. According to Silvio Pampiglione who put it all together the material was assembled on the spot with the help of the "Departamento de Educação e Cultura" of the Liberation Front of Mozambique (Frelimo), the Committee for sanitary aid to the people of Mozambique at Reggio Emilia and the Committee for a free Mozambique at Bologna.

Of extraordinary artistic worth is the disc *Portugal–Angola; chants de lutte*, sung with guitar accompaniment by Luis Cilia (Le Chant du Monde LDX S 4308). A moving expression and experience of human ferocity, misery and hope. The words are provided in Portuguese and French.

Enough (D. Filipe—L. Cilia)[5]

A star,
a bird,
a flower.

A smile,
a child,
a cloud.

A house,
a friend,
an expectation.

---

[5] Of the text the disc gives only the hopeful future and not what is being undergone here and now in the way of cruelty. The complete text can be found in a Dutch translation in "Politieke Poëzie", *Kentering* 12 (1972), n. 4/5, p. 31.

That is enough,
we are going to rebuild the world,
a world of stars, birds, flowers,
smiles, children, clouds,
houses, friends, expectations.

We are in need of a new world,
glad,
simple,
bright,
full of sun.

The Ball (J. Negalha—L. Cilia)

Bleeding
rolls
a ball
over the soil
of Angola.
It is broad daylight
the sun's rays
stream
over the fiery
dust-heap.
Soldiers
play football
with the ball
that bounces
bleeding
on the soil
of Angola.
No one
discerns
in the
dripping
ball
in the sand
that sticks
to the grass

that rolls
over the ground
the bleeding
head
of a black
rolling
over the soil
of Angola.

5. How different in tone are the prayers of free Africans,
which Fritz Pawelzik has collected among the Christians of
Ghana: *Afrika bidt* (The Hague, '1971).

The meal stands steaming hot

O Lord,
the meal stands steaming hot before us on the table
and it smells delicious.
The water to go with it is clear and cool.
We are happy and contented.
But now we are bound to consider
our sisters and brothers
all over the world
who have nothing to eat
and but little to drink.
Be pleased to give your food
and your drink to all.
That is the first thing.
But give them also
what they need, every day,
to carry them through life.
Just as in the wilderness
You gave to the people of Israel
to eat and to drink
give likewise to
our hungry and thirsty brothers,
now and always.
Amen.

6. In the series *Terres de feu* (Paris) various parts are offered

POLITICAL SYMBOLS, POEMS AND SONGS

with poetry: e.g., E. Cardenal, *Cri, psaumes politiques*; M. Dar-wish, *Poèmes Palestiniens; les fleurs du sang*; M. Savarieau (ed.), *Les ancêtres de l'avenir; poèmes révolutionnaires du Guatemala;* H. Vulliez (ed.), *Le tam-tam du sage; Poèmes et proverbes afri-cains.* This series is provided with the following motto: "Is there a country on earth which is not in its own way a 'land of fire'? Everywhere demonstrations, strikes, revolutions, violence. . . . What is that human fire on every horizon? Is it not the ardent hope of a world with its gaze turned towards a peace which it is men's task to build?"

7. We must mention at this point a series of discs, because they are in every respect of exceptional quality: *Le chant du monde* (Le nouveau chansonnier international). The words are printed in the original language with a French translation and the per-formance is perfect.[6]

One is listening here to the new man, who goes through life singing; the man who has some little queries to raise about God, and another, a bit mad, who gets the frogs talking; the one who sings for "his" America, and the poet dreaming in the Moscow underground; the man who testifies or protests; the man who searches, the man who laughs; in a word, people who are really people and have something worthwhile to say.

Brazil: *Ugly* (Carlos Lira)

He is ugly,
He isn't handsome
It's the "morro"
But that will have to stop.

He is singing
But his song is sad
For sadness
Is all he has to sing of.

[6] Known to me in this series are: Argentina (T-LDX 74371, 74394, 74415), Latin America (T-LDX 74395), Brazil (T-LDX 74346), U.S.S.R. (T-LDX 74358), Chile (T-LDX 74407), Uruguay (T-LDX 74362), Italy (T-LDX 74392), U.S.A. (T-LDX 74393), France (T-LDX 74357, 74356), Mexico (T-LDX 74421), Spain (T-LDX 74433), Portugal–Angola (LDX-S 4308), Palestine (LDX 74446).

He is weeping
But as he weeps he laughs
Because he's plucky
And won't squeal.

He loves
The "morro" loves
A lonely loving
A fine loving
That calls for another story.

Chile: *In the Silence of the Night* (Juan Capra)

In the silence of the night
and the noise of the chains
a prisoner was seeking
a cure for his sorrow.

Little bird gaoler,
let me out of this prison
and as price of my freedom
I'll give you my heart.

What does it profit the prisoner
that he has bars made of silver
fetters of gold and pearls,
when he has no freedom.

In the courtyard of the prison
With charcoal it is written:
"The good here grows bad
and the bad even worse."

Uruguay: *The Mass* (César Vallejo—Daniel Viglietti)

At the end of the battle . . .
and the combatant dead, comes to him a man
who says to him: "Don't die; I love you so very much!"
But the corpse, alas, went on with dying.

Two others came up, who said again to him:
"Don't leave us behind! Buck up! Come back to life!"
But the corpse, alas, went on with dying.

Twenty, hundred, a thousand, hundred thousand came to
    him
calling out: "So much love, and nothing to be done about
    death!"
But the corpse, alas, went on with dying.

Millions of people surrounded him
All with the selfsame prayer: "Stay brother!"
But the corpse, alas, went on with dying.

Then, all the people on earth encircled him;
the corpse saw them, was sad and deeply moved;
slowly it stood up,
embraced the first man, and started to walk. . . .

8. The disc *Chants de la Résistance Palestinienne* (LDX 74446)
is introduced with the 7 points of *El Fatah*, the Movement for
National Palestinian Liberation. The orientalist Jean-Claude
Chabrier has produced it. When in 1948 a part of Palestine was
handed over to the Jews, the tribulations began of more than
two million Palestinians in the occupied territory or as refugees
in neighbouring countries, where they were likewise unwelcome.
In 1967 a further bout of suffering ensued for them, and a second
exile. Chabrier got to know the situation in the course of his
travels between 1967 and 1970. The songs of the Fedayin of
Palestine arose in the refugee- and training-camps. They are the
compositions of friendly musicians, creations of anonymous
writers on occasional themes or airs drawn from Palestinian folklore. In the *Assifa*, the *avant-garde* army of the Fatah, the Christian of Nazareth, the Muslim from Jaffa, the man from the occupied district of Bethlehem and the refugee from Irbid have
learned to sing with one voice these melodies of hope. Their songs
are bitter and vehement, rousing and bellicose, repeating catch-
words and slogans like bursts of drumfire.

Assifa (Adaptation by Michel Barbot)

A people under arms,
No more tears!
God defends your cause.
If you should fall
freedom will blossom
upon your grave.
So that this Palestine of ours
may lift her head and live again
we shout, we sing:
Assifa! Assifa!
Assifa! Assifa! Allah Akhbar!
Assifa! Abide in our hearts
for better or for worse!
We shout, we sing:
Assifa! Assifa!

You lead us on the path of honour.
Yes! your name will burn for ever in our hearts.
We all of us follow El Fatah, the vanquisher,
All of us follow El Fatah,
which would, which must, restore to us our good fortune,
to us all, when the scorched earth shall blossom,
All of us follow El Fatah, the vanquisher,
All of us follow El Fatah,
which would, which must, restore to us our good fortune,
to us all, when the scorched earth shall blossom,
Shall blossom . . .

Assifa, abide in our hearts
for better or for worse!
We shout, we sing:
Assifa! Assifa!

9. Thanks to all the propaganda, the songs of Israel are known the world over.[7] They are joyful songs, for Israel has regained her

[7] The following records have been issued under the label *Hed Arzi*: 385. 145 *Shalom Israel zingt*, 576.001/2 *Songs from Israel*, 576.003 *Israel dance*, 576.004 *Kibbutz songs*, 576.005 *Israel army songs*, 576.006 *Famous Israelian Folksongs*.

ancient land and is making it fertile and prosperous. They continue a very long tradition of singing and go right back to the
psalms. Although much is made of the fact that Israel has turned
her back on her God, who has always let his people down, and is
now therefore taking her fate into her own hands, the culture of
the Old Testament survives in the songs, more as a secular than
a sacral experience.

Erev Shel Shoshanim (Evening of roses) is a passage set to
music from the Song of Songs, ending with the words: "... your
mouth in the morning is like a rose; I shall pluck it".—*Lach
Yerushalaïm* (For you, Jerusalem) is an ode to Jerusalem; ". .. between the walls of the city, where a light has arisen, there is in
our hearts one only song, for you, Jerusalem".—*Yerushalaïm
Shel Zahav* was written by Naomi Shemer a few days before the
six-day war and became a hymn of the soldiers who fought to
hold Jerusalem.—*Ani le dodi ve dodi li* (I and my love, my love
and I) is a love song inspired by the Bible: "My love is fair and
has beautiful eyes. We go into the field, and sleep in the vine-
yard; the red of the grape and the beauty of youth".—*Anu hol-
chiem baregel* (We are going on foot) is a "hiking song": "Of
course, it's easier to go by car, but a car can break down. There's
no better way of travellin' than on foot."—*Hineh matov*: "How
good and pleasant a thing it is for brothers to sit down together".
—*Hevenu Shalom Alchem* (We bring you peace) is very popular.

10. There are a lot of discs of Chinese "folk music": Philips
844–935 *Chine* sets modern over against traditional China. We
give here the words of a revolutionary song performed by the
choir of textile factory no. 4 at Sian.

The Red East

The East reddens, the day begins
Above the soil of China Mao Tse Tung rises once more
he works for the wellbeing of the people
He is the saviour of the people.

Mao Tse Tung cherishes the people
He puts us on the right path
To build up the new China
He leads us forward.

The party is our sun
That sheds its brightness everywhere
The moment the party is present
The people have liberty.

11. There are discs also of the songs of Vietnam. Worth noting is Vedette (I Dischi del Vietnam) VPA 8147 *Sulle strade del Vietnam; Registrazioni originali effettuate da Emilio Sarzi Amadè ad Hanoi, Quang Binh, Nam Ha*. What gave occasion for the disc was a long journey through North Vietnam in 1970. In the towns and villages Sarzi Amadè tape-recorded various songs of the people. The recording quality is sometimes imperfect, but the material is highly valuable. The sleeve offers a lengthy description of local conditions, an Italian translation of the words and many photos. What strikes one is the native Vietnamese person's attachment to his bit of land, which he keeps losing and then getting back again. Offered as an example of this is a song from the district of Le Thuy (Beautiful Water) in the Quang Binh province, the most heavily bombed in the whole of Vietnam. This northern province is separated by the river Kien Giang with its "sampans" (fast, narrow boats) and by the political 17th parallel from the provinces of Quang Tri and Thua Tien in the south. It was here that Sarzi Amadè heard the song in which the link with the soil and the landscape is always present, as well as with the enemy, and at the same time the need to defend the heritage conferred by nature and created by man through his labour.

Heroic Le Thuy

Le Thuy lies on both banks of the Kien Giang.
Friends, come and see my land:
The rice-fields and the water wave under the measureless sky.
We have the party to lead us.
We have beaten the enemy.
We have beaten the sky.
Our native soil defies the waves and storms.
We are holding our own:
Tomorrow Binh-Tri-Tien will be reunified.

See the soldiers who make their "sampan" speed smoothly over
  the waves.
The shadow of their guns and the reflected image of the troop
glide over the water under the measureless sky.
With an obstinate love we cherish our native soil.
We shall triumph, for Le Thuy, our native soil,
Continues for ever, on the two banks of the river Kien Giang.

As we bring this documentation, partial though it may be, to
a close, it must be obvious that where symbols, poems and songs
are concerned the meeting between liturgy and politics is an inspiring one. Liturgy, God's being at work for the people, is celebrated not outside but inside the setting where people are. The
locus theologicus is at one and the same time *locus humanus,
locus politicus*, quite concrete towns and villages where people
live and work together, suffer and enjoy themselves, do battle
with the infernal powers on behalf of freedom, justice and peace.
In the term "theology" (and in "anthropology") the Greek word
logos has to be understood in its full meaning. It is a story by
and about God and his People and a living dialogue between God
and men. It is therefore a piece of oratory, and along with that
the business of meditating and reflecting. *Logos* is an interplay of
symbol, poetry, music. God and man declare their love, the one
to the other, a Song of Songs. Around and about God, the angels
sing and we speak of the choirs of angels, give them instruments
of music and join our songs with theirs. The devils have ex-
changed their musical instruments for weapons. Sinful man too
is up in arms. That is why, in the song that humanity sings, the
message is of deliverance from war and violence, wrong and
crime. The songs of the masses—the poor, the tortured and the
slain—are the Christ-song in its most authentic form.

As in the past, so today we encounter living symbols of the
suffering and crucified Christ, prophets with mighty tales to tell,
singers with their songs of protest, scholars with the nerve to
frame theologies of liberation, revolution, black people. As in the
past, these are not always understood and so are persecuted—
which must be so, not only "for the distinguishing of spirits"
and to divide the chaff from the wheat, but also to put to the
proof a truly Christian saying: "through suffering to joy". That

these things must permeate a liturgy that would be truly "of the people" goes without saying; that clashes and conflicts should arise here too is likewise necessary; for good metal is refined in a furnace heat.[8] Man's wrestling with the angel is Christian combat, for the fight to the death ends in the victory of resurrection.

Translated by Hubert Hoskins

[8] A current example is to be found in R. Moccario (ed.). *La communità dell'abata Franzioni*; prefazione di Luigi Bettazzi (Rome, 1973); Giovanni Battista Franzoni, *La terra è di Dio; Lettera pastorale* (COM documenti 1), 1973.

Biographical Notes

Joseph Gelineau, born on 31 October 1920, at Champ-sur-Layon, became a Jesuit in 1941, studying theology at Lyon-Fourvière. He has a diploma in composition and is a doctor of theology of the Institut Catholique at Paris (his thesis was on forms of psalmody in the Syriac Churches of the fourth and fifth centuries), where he teaches pastoral liturgy and liturgical musicology. Both before and since the Council, he has played an active part in the liturgical movement, is the editor of *Église qui chante* and the president of *Universa Laus*. Apart from numerous musical compositions, he has written *Voices and Instruments in Christian Worship* (1965) and many articles in *Maison-Dieu, Études, Concilium*, etc., as well as directing the handbook of pastoral liturgy, *Dans vos Assemblées* (1971).

Joan Llopis was born in Barcelona on 17 July 1932 and ordained in 1958; studied at Salamanca University and at the Gregorian University and the St Anselm Institute of Liturgy, Rome. He has a doctorate in theology and a diploma in psychology and is now professor of liturgy in the theological faculty at Barcelona University and the Pastoral Institute at Madrid. He is a collaborator in the review *Phase* of the Centre of Pastoral Liturgy at Barcelona and is director of the Liturgical Institute there. His publications include *La Sagrada Escritura, fuente de inspiración de la liturgia de difuntos del antiguo rito hispánico* (Barcelona, 1965); *Itinerari litúrgic* (Barcelona, 1968); *La inútil liturgia* (Barcelona, 1972); *El entierro cristiano* (Madrid, 1972).

Hans Bernhard Meyer was born in 1924 at Mannheim, West Germany. He is a Jesuit and was ordained in 1956. He has studied at Freiburg i. Br., Pullach (near Munich), Chantilly (near Paris) and Frankfurt a.M., as well as at St Georgen, Innsbruck and Rome. In Innsbruck he studied under J. A. Jungmann, graduating in 1959. From 1966 to 1969, he was principal of the Institute for Moral Theology and Sociology there and from 1969 onwards director of the department of liturgical science at the Institute of Pastoral Theology. Since 1963, he has been editor-in-chief of the Innsbruck *Zeitschrift für katholische Theologie*. His published works include

"Alkuin zwischen Antike und Mittelalter", *Zeitschrift für katholische Theologie*, 81 (1959), pp. 306–50, 405–54; *Luther und die Messe* (Paderborn, 1965); *Lebendige Liturgie* (Innsbruck, 1966); "Schriftverständnis und Liturgie", *Zeitschrift für katholische Theologie*, 88 (1966), pp. 315–35; "Können wiederverheiratete Geschiedene zu den Sakramenten zugelassen werden?", *Zeitschrift für katholische Theologie*, 91 (1969), pp. 121–49; *Aus Wasser und Geist. Das Sakrament der Taufe und Firmung* (Aschaffenburg, 1969); *Politik im Gottesdienst* (Innsbruck, 1971).

JÜRGEN MOLTMANN, who was born on 8 April 1926 in Hamburg, is a member of the Evangelical Reformed Church. He studied at the University of Göttingen, where he graduated in theology. He was a professor at Wuppertal Theological College 1958–1963, was professor of systematic theology at Bonn University 1963–1967 and is now professor of systematic theology at Tübingen University. He is the editor of *Evangelische Theologie* and has published, among other books and articles, *Prädestination und Perseveranz* (1961), *Theology of Hope* (London, 1967), *Perspektiven der Theologie* (1968), *Der Mensch* (1971) and *Die Ersten Freigelassenen der Schöpfung* (1971²).

JOHN NAVONE was born in Seattle, Washington, in 1930. He entered the Society of Jesus in 1949 and was ordained in 1962. He received his Masters Degree in philosophy from Gonzaga University, Spokane, in 1956. From 1959 to 1963, he studied theology at Regis College in Toronto. In 1963, he was awarded a Masters Degree in Sacred Theology at St Mary's University, Halifax. Since 1967, he has taught theology at the Gregorian University, Rome, and has given summer courses at Seattle University. Among his publications are *History and Faith in the Thought of Dr Alan Richardson* (London, 1966); *Personal Witness: A Biblical Spirituality* (New York, 1967) and *Themes of St Luke* (1970).

DAVID POWER, O.M.I., was born in 1932 in Dublin and ordained in 1956. He studied at the St Anselm Institute of Liturgy, Rome, and is a licentiate in philosophy and doctor of theology. He is now professor of sacramental theology at the Gregorian University, Rome. Among his published works is *Ministers of Christ and His Church* (London, 1969).

HERMAN SCHMIDT was born on 26 June 1912 in Roermond (Netherlands); he joined the Jesuits and became a priest in 1940. He studied at the University of Nijmegen and in Rome at the Oriental Institute, the Institute of Archaeology, the Institute of Sacred Music and the Vatican School of Palaeography. Licentiate in philosophy and doctor of theology, he is professor of liturgy at the Gregorian University and at the St Anselm Institute of Liturgy, Rome. He is a member of the editorial board of the Dutch *Archief van de Kerken* and has published many articles in journals. His books include *Bullarium Anni Sancti* (1949), *Liturgie et langue vulgaire* (1950), *Hebdomada Sancta* (1956–1957), *Introductio in liturgiam occidentalem* (1965³), *Constitutie over de Heilige Liturgie* (1964), *Bidden onderweg van 1960 tot 1970* (1971), *Wie betet der heutige Mensch?* (1972).